Communications in Computer and Information Science   421

T0212897

For further volumes:
http://www.springer.com/series/7899

Asanee Kawtrakul · Dominique Laurent
Nicolas Spyratos · Yuzuru Tanaka (Eds.)

Information Search, Integration, and Personalization

International Workshop, ISIP 2013
Bangkok, Thailand, September 16–18, 2013
Revised Selected Papers

 Springer

Editors
Asanee Kawtrakul
Kasetsart University
Bangkok
Thailand

Nicolas Spyratos
University of Paris South
Orsay
France

Dominique Laurent
Université de Cergy Pontoise
Cergy-Pontoise
France

Yuzuru Tanaka
Hokkaido University
Sapporo
Japan

ISSN 1865-0929 ISSN 1865-0937 (electronic)
ISBN 978-3-319-08731-3 ISBN 978-3-319-08732-0 (eBook)
DOI 10.1007/978-3-319-08732-0
Springer Cham Heidelberg New York Dordrecht London

Library of Congress Control Number: 2014944061

Printed on acid-free paper

Springer is part of Springer Science+Business Media (www.springer.com)

Preface

This book contains the selected research papers presented at ISIP 2013, the 8th International Workshop on Information Search, Integration and Personalization. The workshop was held at Centara Grand & Bangkok Convention Centre, CentralWorld Bangkok, Thailand, during September 16–18, 2013.

In addition to a keynote speech given by Prof. Timos Sellis (RMIT University, Melbourne), there were 28 presentations of scientific papers, of which 24 were submitted to the workshop peer review. The international Program Committee selected ten papers to be included in the proceedings.

The themes of the presented papers reflected the diversity of today's research topics as well as the rapid development of interdisciplinary research. With increasingly sophisticated research in science and technology, there is a growing need for interdisciplinary and international availability, distribution, and exchange of the latest research results, in organic forms, including not only research papers and multimedia documents, but also various tools developed for measurement, analysis, inference, design, planning, simulation, and production as well as the related large data sets. Similar needs are also growing for the interdisciplinary and international availability, distribution, and exchange of ideas and works among artists, musicians, designers, architects, directors, and producers. These contents, including multimedia documents, application tools, and services, are being accumulated on the Web, as well as in local and global databases, at a remarkable speed that we have never experienced with other kinds of publishing media. Large amounts of content are now already on the Web, waiting for their advanced personal and/or public reuse. We need new theories and technologies for the advanced information search, integration through interoperation, and personalization of Web content as well as database content. The ISIP 2013 workshop was organized to offer a forum for presenting original work and stimulating discussions and exchanges of ideas around these themes, focusing on the following topics:

- Information search in large data sets (databases, digital libraries, data warehouses)
- Comparison of different information search technologies, approaches, and algorithms
- Novel approaches to information search
- Personalized information retrieval and personalized Web search
- Data analytics (data mining, data warehousing)
- Integration of Web services, knowledge bases, digital libraries
- Federation of smart objects

ISIP started as a series of Franco-Japanese workshops in 2003, and its first edition was held under the auspices of the French embassy in Tokyo, which provided the financial support along with JSPS (Japanese Society for the Promotion of Science). Up until 2012, the workshops alternated between Japan and France, and attracted increasing interest from both countries. The following list shows the history of past ISIP workshops:

- 2003: First ISIP in Sapporo (June 30–July 2, Meme Media Lab, Hokkaido University)
- 2005: Second ISIP in Lyon (May 9–11, University Claude Bernard Lyon 1)
- 2007: Third ISIP in Sapporo (June 27–30, Meme Media Laboratory, Hokkaido University)
- 2008: 4th ISIP in Paris (Oct. 6–8, Tour Montparnasse, Paris)
- 2009: 5th ISIP in Sapporo (July 6–8, Meme Media Laboratory, Hokkaido University)
- 2010: 6th ISIP in Lyon (Oct. 11–13, University Claude Bernard Lyon 1)
- 2012: 7th ISIP in Sapporo (Oct. 11–13, Meme Media Lab, Hokkaido University)

Originally, the workshops were intended for a Franco-Japanese audience, with the occasional invitation of researchers from other countries as keynote speakers. The proceedings of each workshop were published informally, as a technical report of the hosting institution. One exception was the 2005 workshop, selected papers of which were published by the *Journal of Intelligent Information Systems* in its special issue for ISIP 2005 (Vol. 31, Number 2, October 2008). The original goal of the ISIP workshop series was to create close synergies between a selected group of researchers from the two countries; and indeed, several collaborations, joint publications, joint student supervisions, and research projects originated from participants of the workshop.

After the first six workshops, the organizers concluded that the workshop series had reached a mature state with an increasing number of researchers participating every year. As a result, the organizers decided to open up the workshop to a larger audience by inviting speakers from over ten countries at ISIP 2012 as well as at ISIP 2013. The effort to attract an even larger international audience will continue in the years to come.

The selected papers contained in this book are grouped into three major topics, namely, Knowledge Federation and Integration, Information Discovery, and Recommendation Systems and Ontologies.

We would like to express our appreciation to all speakers and participants of ISIP 2013 for their intensive discussions and exchange of new ideas. This book is an outcome of those discussions and ideas.

January 2014

Asanee Kawtrakul
Nicolas Spyratos
Yuzuru Tanaka

Organization

ISIP 2013 was organized by the Department of Computer Engineering of the Kasetsart University, Bangkok, Thailand.

Executive Committee

Co-chairs

Asanee Kawtrakul   Kasetsart University, Thailand
Nicolas Spyratos   Paris-Sud University, France
Yuzuru Tanaka   Hokkaido University, Japan

Program Committee Co-chairs

Dominique Laurent   University of Cergy-Pontoise, France
Tetsuya Yoshida   Hokkaido University, Japan
Vilas Wuwongse   Thammasat University, Thailand
Phuchong Uthayophak   Kasetsart University, Thailand

Local Organization

Asanee Kawtrakul   Kasetsart University, Thailand
Chularat Tanprasert   NECTEC, Thailand

Publication

Siriporn Ongroungrueng   Kasetsart University, Thailand
Mukda Suktarachan   Kasetsart University, Thailand
Marut Buranarach   NECTEC, Thailand

Program Committee

M. Adriani	J. Darmont	K.P. Jantke
M. Akaishi	J. Fujima	A. Kawtrakul
H. Arimura	K. Furukawa	M. Kitsuregawa
M. Buranarach	R. Goebel	D. Kotzinos
H. Chanlekha	M.-S. Hacid	H. L. Larsen
Ch. Chantrapornchai	M. Haraguchi	A. Laurent
R. Chbeir	K. Imai	D. Laurent
P. Chongstitvatana	H. Imura	C. Meghini
Y.-W. Choong	K. Ito	Sh. Minato
V. Christophides	M. Itoh	J. Mitrpanont

Contents

Knowledge Federation and Integration

Geospatial Digital Dashboard
for Exploratory Visual Analytics

Jonas Sjöbergh$^{(\boxtimes)}$ and Yuzuru Tanaka

Meme Media Lab, Hokkaido University, Sapporo, Japan
{js,tanaka}@meme.hokudai.ac.jp

Abstract. We present a system for visual data exploration, built using pluggable software components, which allows ad hoc combination of data from different sources ("data mash-up"). Interaction is done through "direct manipulation", making it easy to use for domain experts that may not be data mining or computer experts. All visualized results can be interacted with, and selections or groupings using one visualization result are automatically reflected in all other views of the same data.

1 Introduction

There are now many sources of "big data". Cheap storage and cheap sensors has made it possible to collect many types of data in huge quantities. With social networking, users in large numbers are also producing large amounts of user generated content. Examples of "big data" that it is now possible to get access to include: publicly collected data such as weather data, traffic records (accident records, traffic jam data), tracking data such as records of credit card usage, mobile phone location, car location (from the GPS navigation system), social networking data such as location tagged photos or short texts, and much more.

Combining different data sources can give insights not available using only one source, and different data sources can cover for each other when data becomes unavailable from one source.

We are currently involved in a project on using big data to help with disaster management, and in particular to help with snow removal in the city of Sapporo. Sapporo is a big city that gets very large amounts of snow every year, which is similar to a regularly occurring small natural disaster. We hope to improve the snow plowing and removing strategies by using "big data".

Big data is normally so big that it is difficult for a human to get a grip of the information in the data. Using data mining and statistical methods to extract the information we are interested in is one way to use big data. Sometimes, it is not obvious what information we want or how to extract the information we need from a set of data sources. Visualizing the data to a user can then help in getting ideas of what data to extract or how to process the data further.

When something out of the ordinary, like a natural disaster, happens, it is not always clear what data contains the information we want. The ideal data

A. Kawtrakul et al. (Eds.): ISIP 2013, CCIS 421, pp. 3–17, 2014.
DOI: 10.1007/978-3-319-08732-0_1, © Springer International Publishing Switzerland 2014

may also not be accessible to us at such times, and we may thus need to use other sources of data and do the best we can using these.

To help in situations such as when you do not know how to model your problem or when you have to access new unfamiliar data sources, we have developed an environment for visual exploration of data. It allows many types of visualizations of many types of data, and it allows ad hoc federation of different data sources (data mash-up) and adding of new visualization methods.

2 Snow Removal Project

In our project we are interested in using many sources of data to help dealing with snow in the winter here in Sapporo, and with disaster management in general. Sapporo is a city in northern Japan with 1.9 million citizens and an annual snowfall of about 6 m. Plowing roads and removing snow to keep the city working during the winter is a big problem and costs about 147 million dollars per year. It is similar to a small natural disaster that occurs regularly, and can be used to try out disaster management strategies etc.

We have access to many sources of data, including:

- Probe car data, around 2000 taxis driving in Sapporo giving their time, location, and speed. We also have similar data from private cars, but the number of sensor enabled private cars is much lower.
- Traffic jam sensor data, from traffic jam sensors all over Sapporo.
- Multi-sensor weather data, measurements of wind, temperature, rain, snowfall, snow depth on the ground, moisture, etc. at 52 locations in and around the city. We also have weather radar data from a different source.
- Snow plowing and snow removal records. Data collected by hand by the companies that remove snow.
- Snow related call center complaints. Data collected by call center operators answering calls from citizens reporting snow related problems or complaining about the snow removal service.
- Subway data, the number of passengers entering and leaving each subway station of the three subway lines in the city.
- Traffic accident reports, collected by the police.
- Social networking data, time and location stamped texts from Sapporo from users of the Twitter social networking service.

One part of the project is building a library of tools to visualize/explore these data. A system for doing this is described in the next section. An older version of this system, as well as other things that are being done in the project, have been described elsewhere [1].

3 Digital Dashboard for Visual Data Exploration

The *Digital Dashboard* is a system for visual exploration of data. It allows visualization of data from many sources at the same time, using many types of visualization methods. The user interface is based on "direct manipulation", and all visualization components are expected to allow manipulation of the visualization results. The direct manipulation can for instance be clicking and dragging on a map to select areas, clicking on representations of subsets of data in a clustering component, etc.

The *Digital Dashboard* is built using components. There are components for interfacing with data sources of various kinds, and components for visualizing data. The *Dashboard* provides a simple interface for components to connect to it (and expects all components to support a simple interface) and hides the components from each other. An individual component does not need to know anything about the data source components its data comes from or about other visualization components that are currently visualizing the same data, it only needs to interact with the *Dashboard*.

The *Dashboard* and its components are built using the *Webble World* framework [2], the latest version of the *Meme Media (IntelligentPad)* framework [3]. A *Webble* is a pluggable software component.

3.1   Webble Technology

The goal of *Meme Media* is to make functionality and services as easy to reuse as copy-pasting texts or images is today. *Meme Media Webbles* are intelligent pluggable software components that exist on the Web. The *Webble* technology allows wrapping existing software with interface wrappers and once some software has been wrapped it can be used together with other *Webbles*, and used/reused in many applications. *Webbles* can of course also be written from scratch.

The *Webble World* framework is currently implemented in Silverlight, and *Webble* software runs in any Web browser that has a Silverlight plugin. Currently, a new version of the *Webble World* framework is being built using HTML5 and Javascript instead of Silverlight, which will allow *Webbles* to run on many more platforms, such as mobile devices.

In the *Digital Dashboard* there are components written from scratch, components that wrap previously existing *Webbles* to conform to the interface expected by the *Dashboard*, and components that wrap previously existing external software. One example of the latter is a *Webble* that displays geospatial information on a map, which was built by wrapping the ArcGIS[1] software with a *Webble* wrapping interface.

Webbles (and *IntelligentPads*) communicate using *slots*. A *slot* is an access point to a variable or method in the *Webble*, and *Webbles* that are connected to each other can have *slots* connected too. These *slots* will then exchange values whenever the value of one *slot* is changed, effectively making a variable a shared variable between the two *Webbles*.

3.2   Dashboard Internal Structure and Component Interface

The *Digital Dashboard* has three types of components, the *Digital Dashboard* parent component, visualization components, and data source components.

---

[1] ESRI (2012) ArcGIS API for Silverlight (ver. 2.4),
   http://help.arcgis.com/en/webapi/silverlight/.

New components can be built and plugged in at any time, even when the system is already running. As long as they conform to the simple interface expected by the *Dashboard* parent, they can be used as soon as they are plugged in.

Each component is plugged into the *Dashboard* parent, but the components have no knowledge of other components that may be running. All communication between components, such as sending the data from a data source component to a visualization component, goes through the *Dashboard*. Components can have (*Webble*) children of their own, as for example the *Map Interaction* component that acts as an adapter between the *Dashboard* and a previously existing *Webble* for using the ArcGIS framework.

All components plugged into the *Dashboard* are expected to have two *slots*: PluginName (specifying what this component should be called in menus etc.) and PluginType (specifying whether it is a visualization component or a data source component). The different types of components are then expected to have further *slots*, specific to the component type.

The data source components hide the underlying data storage format from the *Dashboard*. Data source components can for example be *Webbles* that allow access to an SQL database and return the data in the format expected by the *Dashboard*, *Webbles* that parse XML files, or *Webbles* that access Web services.

Data source components are expected to follow a simple interface. They are expected to have the following *slots*:

- ProvidedFormat, and XML string specifying what data this source provides. It details the data types of the different data fields, and what these fields should be called (in menus etc.).
- FormatChanged, signaling that the format of the data this source provides has changed.
- DataValuesChange, signaling that the data has changed and the parent needs to update any visualization components using data from this source.

They also have *slots* containing the actual data, one *slot* for each data field. The data is stored as vectors, so numerical data would be stored as a vector of doubles (or integers) and text data would be stored as a vector of strings, etc. These *slots* are described in the XML of the ProvidedFormat *slot*.

Visualization components are expected to have the following *slots*:

- ExpectedFormat, and XML describing what types of data the plugin expects and in which *slots* it expects to received the data.
- FormatChanged, signalling that the component has changed what types of data it expects.
- DataValuesSetFilled, as slot where the parent informs the plugin about which slots it has filled with data (some data fields could be optional, or several different sets of data could be allowed, etc.).
- DataValuesChanged, a slot where the parent signals that the data has changed and the plugin should parse the new data etc.
- LocalSelections, a slot where the plugin tells the parent which data items are selected/deselected/grouped together on this component.

- GlobalSelections, a slot where the parent tells the plugin the global selection status of the data items (e.g. a data item may be selected locally on one plugin but unselected on another component, making it unselected in total).
- GroupColors, information on what colors the plugins should use to visualize different groups of data (to get a uniform look across all components).

They also have *slots* for data input, similar to the *slots* for data output in the data source components, expecting vectors of strings etc. These are described in the XML of the ExpectedFormat *slot*.

In an older version of the *Digital Dashboard*, the component interface was slightly different. The older version used XML to pass data between data sources and components, while the current version uses vectors of primitive data types (or objects, for more complicated data types). The XML version had a cleaner interface, but generating and parsing XML for a lot of the communication turned out to be too slow when using the system on big data. A description of the previous interface can be found in [4].

Derived attributes can be computed at runtime and used for selecting subsets of data etc. One example is a clustering component that clusters data and then allows grouping and selecting data based on which cluster they belong to.

3.3   Usage Example

The *Digital Dashboard* is intended to work for visualizing and exploring any type of data, but since it is being developed in a project with focus on snow removal the first components developed are components that are helpful for data that may help with that. Since a lot of the information is geographic in nature, there is for instance a component that visualizes geographic data on a map. It could for instance be useful to show roads where the speed is currently lower than normal (perhaps caused by snow or ice) or locations of recent traffic accidents. A quick look could then give an indication of if there are areas that seem to have more problems than others, or if snow removal resources are currently limited, which areas to prioritize etc.

In Fig. 1 an example of what the *Digital Dashboard* looks like is shown, showing one of the many setups possible. There are six visualization plugins and one data source plugin used in the example setup. There are also two other *Webbles* that are connected to one of the visualization components.

The data source component contains probe car data. The data is statistically treated data that originates from about 2,000 taxis driving around the city and reporting the time, location, and speed when they pass traffic lights. The data is then averaged for each road segment in the city, where a road segment is basically a stretch of road between two traffic lights or intersections. For each road segment the data contains statistical data for each five minutes period during each day. The data available for each segment and each five minutes period are: the minimum, maximum, and average speed; the time; the number of taxis (of the probe car taxis) with passengers in them that passed. The data also contains the location of the road segments, their lengths, etc.

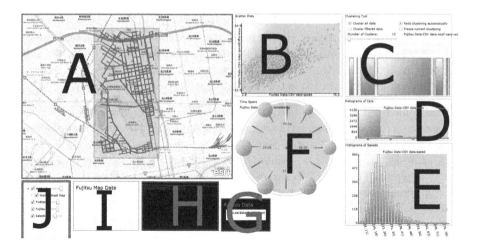

Fig. 1. The *Digital Dashboard* showing probe car data: time stamped traffic amount and speed readings for road segments. **A** is an ArcGIS map *Webble*, **B** is a scatter plot visualization component, **C** is a clustering component, **D** and **E** are two instances of a histogram component, **F** is a 24 h clock component, **G** is the probe car data source component, **H** is the *Dashboard* parent *Webble*, **I** is a visualization component using the map *Webble* **A**, and **J** is a *Webble* to hide or make layers on the map transparent.

The example setup shows a one day subset of the data from a winter day, and only from road segments around our university. The data is collected for every day, and all road segments in the city (over 100,000 road segments). In the example setup the data has been further averaged over four hour periods.

The visualization components used in the example setup are: a 24 h clock to select time segments (**F**); two instances of a component showing histograms, here showing the average speeds and the average number of cars per five minutes (**D** and **E**); a scatter plot component, showing the average speed on the horizontal axis and the speed on this winter day compared to the average speed of the same road segment in the summer (the "winter speed down") (**B**); a clustering component that shows clusters that the component created by clustering the road segments based on 288 dimensional (24 hours × 12 five minute periods per hour) vectors of the number of cars passing during the day (**C**); a map visualization component showing the road segments on top of a map of Sapporo (**I**). The last component uses an ArcGIS wrapper *Webble* to show maps (**A**), which in turn uses a *Webble* for controlling the layers on the map (**J**).

A simple example of interacting with the components is shown in Fig. 2. In the upper image, component **D** was used to select only roads with a lot of taxi traffic. All other data items are automatically removed from all components visualizing the same data. The road segments still shown in green on the map correspond to the main roads around the university, as expected.

Data can also be divided into different groups and contrasted against each other. In the lower part of Fig. 2, the clustering component (**C**) was used to divide

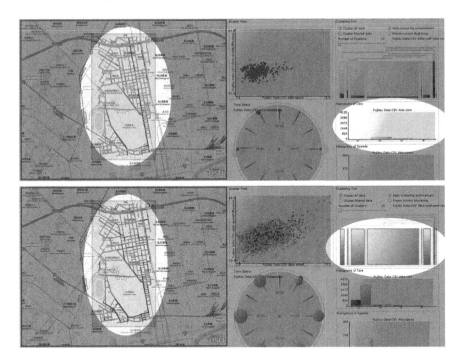

Fig. 2. Selecting road segments with a lot of traffic in two different ways (Color figure online).

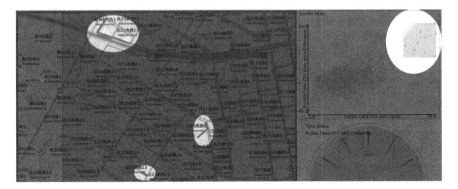

Fig. 3. A closer look at segments with speed outliers.

the data into two groups based on the clustering result. Since the clustering was based on the amount of traffic throughout the day, the green group still corresponds well with the main roads around the university.

In Fig. 3 the scatter plot has been used to select road segments with speed outliers, segments where the average speed was unusually high. The map has been zoomed in on a few of these to take a closer look. Some segments are

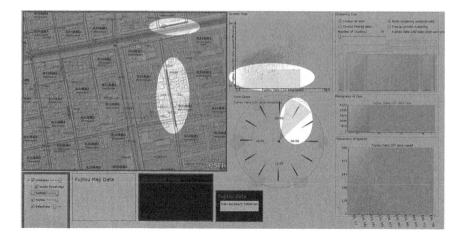

Fig. 4. A closer look at segments with potential snow or ice problems.

stretches of the expressway through Sapporo, which naturally has a high average speed. Other road segments are mostly very short road segments with little traffic. A guess is that the high speeds are taxis rushing to pass a changing traffic light, which would give a large increase in the average speed if the segment is short and there are no other taxis there during the same time interval.

To find areas that may be in need of snow removal, we can select road segments that have a large speed difference compared to the average speed in the summer (at the same time of day and the same day of the week). A histogram component could be used to show such data and select road segments like that. In Fig. 4 the scatter plot, which shows the speeds and the speed difference compared to the summer average speeds, is used to select road segments with large speed downs. The 24 h clock is also used to show only segments where the problems persist at night. If there are large speed downs even at night, when traffic is low, the cause is often ice making the road slippery or snow making the road narrow or in other ways difficult to use. The map has then been zoomed in on an area with several road segments with problems clustered together.

Since we do not know what caused the speed downs in the areas, it might be helpful to add data from a different source as a complement. In Fig. 5, a data source component with data from the Twitter social networking service has been added. The data contains the text content, the time stamp, and the GPS location of a number of tweets from inside Sapporo on the same day as the probe care data already visualized.

One more instance of the map visualization component has also been added, to show the Twitter data on the map. In the upper image of Fig. 5, the map has been zoomed out and we can see that most tweets are sent in the city center, as is to be expected since this is the area with the most people during the day.

In the lower image, the map visualization component has been used to select only tweets containing the word "the". This is a quick way to select tweets in

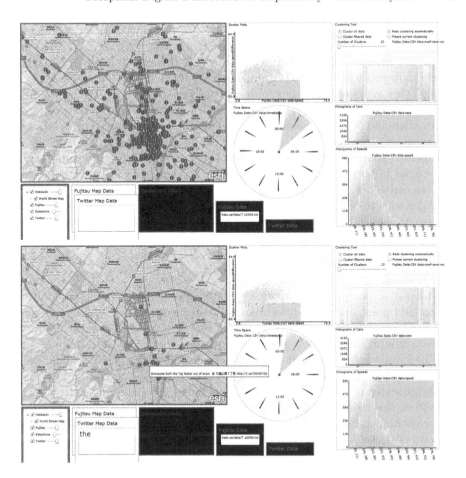

Fig. 5. Adding data from Twitter, and filtering these data to show tweets in English.

English (most of which contain "the") and remove tweets in Japanese. Most Sapporo citizens write in Japanese on Twitter, and the remaining tweets are mainly tweets by tourists visiting the city. The tweets from the tourists are heavily concentrated to the city center, to the main street in Susukino and to the big Odori park in the middle of Sapporo. The day these data were collected was the first day of the Sapporo Snow Festival, which is located in the Odori park and draws huge amounts of tourists (around 2 million people per year) and of the Susukino Ice Festival, located in the Susukino area. The tourist tweets thus occur where you would expect them to occur, and checking the text content by hovering the mouse over a tweet we can see the Snow Festival related: "Someone built the Taj Mahal out of snow".

We can check this data to see if someone is mentioning snow, ice, slipperiness, etc. near the road segments that seemed to have problems, but on this day there were no such tweets. The road segments around the festival areas also have huge speed downs during the day (when the festival area is open) and some road segments are even closed off during certain hours these days. If you were not already aware of the Snow Festival, checking the tweets in the area would quickly show you why these road segments have unusual data during these days. Adding other types of data from sources could also give more insights.

Apart from the simple usage examples shown above, all components can also be moved around (by clicking and dragging) to put visualization results you want together near each other. The components can be resized to see more details in a component you care more about and to waste less screen space on components that are not important for the moment. More components can be added at any time (as can other *Webbles*), and components can of course also be removed. The color scheme of the components and the colors used for the visualized data can also be changed easily through the *Dashboard* parent.

4   Similar Systems

Here we give a short overview of other systems for visualization and exploration of data, and point out some differences between them and our system.

RapidMiner [5] is an open-source prototyping system for knowledge discovery and data mining. It is widely used and supports very many data mining and machine learning algorithms. It is used to graphically set up work flows for data mining. It supports multiple views of the same data and you can go back and change some step of the work flow and get a different visualization results. Like in our system, the underlying data format is hidden from the data mining operators or visualization components, and changes made to a work flow are reflected in all views of those data. The interaction when setting up work flows is a visual process, but, there is no interaction with the visualized results.

Snap-Together Visualization [6] (*Snap*) is very similar to our system. Different visualization components are connected and e.g. selecting data in one component is automatically reflected in connected components. As in our system the interaction can be bidirectional so interactions with the second component are reflected in the first component too. Components can be connected in different ways, so selecting an item may select related items in one connected view, and open details about the selected item in another view. *Snap*, like our system, has a small interface that components need to follow and it is possible to wrap existing software with an interface wrapper (in for instance Visual Basic). Unlike our system, *Snap* expects the data to come from a database (supporting ODBC) and uses Microsoft's COM for component (process) communication.

The *VERD* [7] system uses IntelligentBox, another version of *Meme Media* [3], for data visualization. It works with relational databases and has a wrapper to treat Web resources as relational schema too. Using direct manipulation, it allows interactive data exploration using various visualization methods. All visualization views set up are also treated as relations, making it possible to apply the same operations to visualization views as to raw data. *VERD* requires the IntelligentBox environment while our system runs in any Web browser, and in *VERD* the interaction only goes downstream in the visualization flow, i.e. interaction with one component does not affect components earlier in the flow.

DEVise [8] is a data exploration system for relational databases. It supports multiple views that can be connected so that e.g. zooming in one view is reflected in another view, and connections can be bidirectional. *DEVise* supports many types of operations on the data, but the types of user interaction with the visualization results are somewhat limited.

Tioga-2 [9] (now called *Tioga DataSplash*) is a direct manipulation system for setting up visualizations of database contents. Multiple visualizations can be connected and changes in the range to visualize in one are then automatically reflected in others. *Tioga* has a fairly limited set of visualization primitives and only works with relational databases as the data source.

The *Trial Outline Builder* [10] (*TOB*) can be considered an older version of the *Digital Dashboard*. The *TOB* is a system for supporting clinical trials on cancer and can generate trial design plans (flow charts) and help with collecting data. It also has a data analysis part, built with components similar to the *Digital Dashboard* components, though they were written specifically for *TOB* and were not generic. They were built using *Webbles*, so they can easily be integrated into the *Dashboard*, though.

4.1 Available Components and Performance

The *Digital Dashboard* can be set up using any combination of the available components and the usage example in the previous section only shows one small example. New components are built when a need arises, so the number of available components is not fixed.

Currently the following data source components are available:

– XML Data Source, a data source component that parses XML files containing data and converts the data to the format expected by the *Dashboard* parent. Can be used together with existing *Webbles* that allow accessing Web Services to use Web Services providing data in XML format.
– CSV Data Source, a data source component that parses CSV (Comma Separated Vector) data files (used by many available data manipulating software, for example Excel) and converts the data to the format expected by the *Dashboard* parent.

There are also a number of visualization components available. Many instances of the same visualization component (or data source component) can be used at the same time, i.e. you can have several Bar Chart components, showing different data fields. Currently the following visualization components are available:

– Bar Charts, visualizes data using histograms or bar charts.
– Scatter Plots, visualizes two dimensional data as a scatter plot.
– Text Statistics, shows e.g. histograms of the most common words in text data.
– Clock, visualizes time data on a 12 or 24 h clock.

– Point Data on Maps, visualizes geospatial data as points on maps (e.g. weather stations, or sent Twitter messages).
– Line Data on Maps, visualizes geospatial data as lines on maps (e.g. road segments).
– Trajectories on Maps, visualizes series of geospatial data on a map as points connected by lines (e.g. all Tweets by the same user ordered by time).
– Clustering, clusters vector data using various clustering algorithms, visualizes the clustering results, and allows selection or grouping of data items based on the clustering results.
– Life Tables, visualizes data as "Life Tables", survivability charts. Plots the number of data items (normally patients) that remain in a group (e.g. are still alive, or still relapse free) as a function of time (e.g. the number of weeks after being diagnosed). Frequently used to show or compare the efficacy of medical treatments.
– Storygraphs, visualizing geospatial data over time using Storygraphs [11]. These are visualizations where the horizontal axis is time, the left hand vertical axis is the latitude, and the right hand side vertical axis is the longitude. A data item is drawn on the line from its latitude to its longitude, at the point corresponding to its time.
– Parallel Coordinates, visualizes multi dimensional data using parallel coordinates [12], where coordinate axes are lined up beside each other and a point in the multi dimensional space becomes a series of line segments between the data axes.

All visualization components also allow interaction, so you can select or group data items by selecting bars in a bar chart, by selecting frequent words, by selecting areas on a map, by selecting time slices on a clock, etc.

Performance-wise, the more visualization components you use at the same time, the slower the visualization becomes. The main cost is that since there are more components that draw things, there are more things to draw and thus the time spent drawing on the screen is increased. The cost for the *Dashboard* parent coordinating more components is very low compared to the cost of drawing on the screen.

Some visualization components are much more performance intensive than others. It is for instance much more costly to draw dots representing each individual Twitter message on a map than it is to draw a histogram of how many messages were sent each day, since there are so many dots to draw on the map (the locations of the messages do not overlap very often, so the number of dots will be close to the number of messages) compared to drawing just a few rectangles for each day. Adding many more visualization components that do not draw that much on the screen does not impact the performance noticeably, while adding just a single component that is slow will have a large impact. Most components are written so as to only do incremental updates of the graphics (only redraw things that have changed), so once the initial visualization is done the system can be very fast as long as you do not do large changes in each step (e.g. deselect almost all data).

The amount of data that is being visualized also has a large impact on the performance, of course. The number of different data sources used does not have a large performance impact, but the total amount of data, or more precisely the amount of graphical elements that end up on screen, has a large impact.

The *Digital Dashboard* is still under development and has not been heavily optimized for performance. Currently, visualizing 4,000 traffic accidents using 10 different visualization components on a standard desktop computer is very responsive. All the visuals are updated in real time as soon as subsets of data are selected on any component or the data is grouped in new ways. Visualizing 4.5 megabytes of taxi probe car data using 10 different visualization components is fast (everything is immediately updated) if you make small changes (e.g. select small areas on the map) but when redrawing all visualizations (e.g. changing between selecting almost all data and almost no data) it takes a few seconds to update the graphics. Most of this time is spent redrawing the lines representing the road segments on the map.

5   Discussion

Using the *Meme Media* component based framework to build the system makes development and prototyping very fast. The *Dashboard* hiding the components from each other and only requiring a simple interface also makes it easy to develop new components. A wrapper to make existing *Webbles* work with the *Dashboard* can be written in a few hours, and writing a new component from scratch usually takes from one to a few days (depending on what the functionality of the component is).

The *Meme Media* also makes it easy to reuse software, and several of the components in our system have already been reused in other systems. We have incorporated components developed for other systems in the *Dashboard* too.

Making the *Dashboard* component interface generic and having all communication go through the *Dashboard* does make some things slower, and tightly integrating all components could make the system more efficient. A previous version of our system used XML as a cleaner and more generic way for components to communicate, but this turned out to be too slow to make the system interactive when visualizing big data. We believe the current design is a good compromise between run time efficiency and development speed and reusability.

Using direct manipulation as the main interaction method makes the system easy to use for users with little knowledge of computers or data mining. This means that users with domain knowledge (such as snow removal professionals in our case, or cancer specialists in another project we are involved in) can use the system and at the same time make use of their expertise in the field.

That all visualization results can be interacted with has been well received by users in the target audience (snow removal specialists, cancer researchers, etc.). It is powerful that you can use the visualization that tells you some subset of the data looks interesting directly to further refine your exploration.

Another thing that has been well received is that all views of the same data are automatically updated when selections or groupings in one view of the data are changed. It is possible to set up unconnected views of the same data too, if you want both types of behavior.

Derived attributes calculated from the data at run time can also be used like normal attributes in the system. Currently there is a clustering tool that clusters the data and you can then use the cluster ID together with other attributes to do further selections in the data. We are also building a pattern mining tool, other machine learning tools, and some statistical analysis tools, though these were not detailed in this paper.

6   Conclusions

We described a system based on pluggable software components. It allows ad hoc data exploration/visualization and ad hoc combination of data sources.

Interaction is done through "direct manipulation", which is intuitive and easy for non-experts (on data mining etc.) to use. All visualization results can also be interacted with, and selections or groupings based on one visualization result automatically update all other visualizations of the same data.

The component based technology used to build the system allows for fast prototyping, and it makes the ad hoc addition of new data sources or new visualization components easy.

References

1. Tanaka, Y., Sjöbergh, J., Moiseets, P., Kuwahara, M., Imura, H., Yoshida, T.: Geospatial visual analytics of traffic and weather data for better winter road management. In: Cervone, G., Lin, J., Waters, N. (eds.) Data Mining for Geoinformatics. Springer, New York (2014)
2. Kuwahara, M., Tanaka, Y.: Webble world-a Web-based knowledge federation framework for programmable and customizable Meme Media objects. In: The IET International Conference on Frontier Computing 2010, Taichung, Taiwan, pp. 372–377 (2010)
3. Tanaka, Y.: Meme Media and Meme Market Architecture. IEEE Press, Piscataway (2003)
4. Sjöbergh, J., Tanaka, Y.: Visual data exploration using webbles. In: Arnold, O., Spickermann, W., Spyratos, N., Tanaka, Y. (eds.) WWS 2013. CCIS, vol. 372, pp. 119–128. Springer, Heidelberg (2013)
5. Mierswa, I., Wurst, M., Klinkenberg, R., Scholz, M., Euler, T.: YALE: rapid prototyping for complex data mining tasks. In: Proceedings of the 12th ACM SIGKDD, KDD'06, Philadelphia, PA, USA, pp. 935–940 (2006)
6. North, C., Shneiderman, B.: Snap-together visualization: a user interface for coordinating visualizations via relational schemata. In: Proceedings of AVI'00, Palermo, Italy, pp. 128–135 (2000)
7. Sugibuchi, T., Tanaka, Y.: Integrated visualization framework for relational databases and web resources. In: Proceedings of IHI'04, Dagstuhl Castle, Germany, pp. 159–174 (2004)

8. Livny, M., Ramakrishnan, R., Beyer, K., Chen, G., Donjerkovic, D., Lawande, S., Myllymaki, J., Wenger, K.: DEVise: integrated querying and visual exploration of large datasets. In: Proceedings of SIGMOD'97, Tucson, AZ, USA, pp. 301–312 (1997)
9. Aiken, A., Chen, J., Stonebraker, M., Woodruff, A.: Tioga-2: a direct manipulation database visualization environment. In: Proceedings of ICDE'96, New Orleans, LA, USA, pp. 208–217 (1996)
10. Sjöbergh, J., Kuwahara, M., Tanaka, Y.: Visualizing clinical trial data using pluggable components. In: Proceedings of the 16th International Conference on Information Visualisation, IV'2012, Montpellier, France, pp. 291–296 (2012)
11. Shrestha, A., Zhu, Y., Miller, B., Zhao, Y.: Storygraphs: extracting patterns from spatio-temporal data. In: Proceedings of IDEA'13, Chicago, IL, USA, pp. 96–104 (2013)
12. Inselberg, A., Dimsdale, B.: Parallel coordinates: a tool for visualizing multi-dimensional geometry. In: Proceedings of the 1st conference on Visualization '90, VIS'90, Los Alamitos, CA, USA, pp. 361–378 (1990)

Authoring Composite Documents and Their Descriptions

Nicolas Spyratos and Tsuyoshi Sugibuchi[✉]

Laboratoire de Recherche en Informatique, Université Paris-Sud 11, Orsay, France
Nicolas.Spyratos@lri.fr,
tsuyoshi.sugibuchi@internetmemory.net

Abstract. We present a method for describing composite documents based on the descriptions of their components. Our main objective is to assist authors of composite documents in selecting documents and their descriptions during the authoring process. We assume that a document description is a set of terms from a given taxonomy, such that no two terms in the set are comparable. We call such a description a "reduced description" and we show that the set of all reduced descriptions forms a complete lattice under an appropriate ordering. Based on this lattice we introduce the concept of "admissible description" and we argue that admissible descriptions are the only ones that describe composite documents in a useful and meaningful manner.

1 Introduction

Today's growth of digital publishing is bringing about not only media migration from atom to bit, but also more flexibility in authoring and customizing digital documents *after* their publication. For example, several non-profit projects and commercial companies start to offer *open textbook* platforms that intend to allow textbook authors, educators and students to create and customize textbooks. An interesting example is the *Connexions project* [1] funded by Rice University. In the Connexions' repository, every textbook is managed as a collection of individual learning objects called *modules*. The Connexions' website allows users not only to read textbooks but also to create and customize textbooks by composing modules taken from a variety of existing textbooks.

To make a new textbook by composing fragments of existing textbooks, authors need to find appropriate fragments from textbook repositories. At present, most open textbook platforms adopt description based document management. In such systems, each document and its fragments are associated with *descriptions*, also called *metadata*, two terms that we shall use interchangeably in the rest of the paper. Usually metadata contains free-text information including title, short description and free keywords, and information based on controlled vocabularies, or *taxonomies*, including subject category, topic group, etc. We note here that when the terms of a controlled vocabulary are hierarchically organized, then the controlled vocabulary is usually called a *taxonomy*.

A. Kawtrakul et al. (Eds.): ISIP 2013, CCIS 421, pp. 18–30, 2014.
DOI: 10.1007/978-3-319-08732-0_2, © Springer International Publishing Switzerland 2014

Information based on controlled vocabularies is useful for more accurate and intelligent content retrieval, if metadata is properly created and maintained.

If we intend to allow users to take fragments from textbooks with smaller granularity, the cost of authoring metadata for each textbook fragment might be a problem. In particular, if authors have 100 % freedom of selection of terms for metadata, it rather makes metadata authoring tasks more difficult because authors need to choose terms without any clues. However, if we can define formal criteria of "better" or "consistent" descriptions, the story becomes slightly different. In this case, authoring systems can automatically check the current descriptions and give "suggestions" to authors to improve the descriptions. The main goal of this study is twofold: (a) to capture, and state formally, some simple but practically important requirements of descriptions, and (b) to demonstrate how to use them to help authors make good descriptions with less effort.

To this end, we propose a simple metadata management model for document composition environments. Our model assumes that (a) composite documents are structured as trees, whose nodes are either atomic documents, or other composite documents and (b) descriptions of documents are sets of terms taken from a taxonomy. The model does not consider contents of documents but deals only with their composition structure and the descriptions associated with the components of a composite document in order to *infer* appropriate descriptions (for the composite document).

Our basic assumption is that a document description is a set of terms from a given taxonomy, such that no two terms in the set are comparable. We call such a description a "reduced description". In adopting this definition, our goal is to ensure that documents are described in a non redundant way and that, consequently, they can be retrieved more efficiently. We show that the set of all reduced descriptions forms a complete lattice under an appropriate ordering. Based on this lattice we introduce the concept of "admissible description" and we argue that admissible descriptions are the only (reduced) descriptions that describe composite documents in a useful and meaningful manner. We also outline an interactive process to assist users in authoring composite documents and choosing a desirable admissible description. We emphasize that the ultimate choice of a description is up to the document author and that the work presented here aims simply to assist the author in making an informed choice.

In the rest of the paper we first review some related studies (Sect. 2). Then we present our model for documents and their descriptions, as well as algorithms for description inference (Sect. 3). Based on this model, we introduce the concept of "admissible description" and outline an interactive process to assist users in authoring composite documents and choosing a desirable admissible description (Sect. 4).

2 Related Work and Preliminary Concepts

A lot of efforts have been devoted recently to develop languages and tools to generate, store and query metadata. Some of the most noticeable achievements are the RDF language, RDF schema and several standards for representing controlled vocabularies, including OWL [4] and SKOS [5]. By using such languages and standards, several controlled vocabularies for metadata have been developed and are widely used in practice. These vocabularies include the ACM Computing Classification System [6] (for computer science), Gene Ontology [7] (genomics), AAT [8] (arts and architectures), DBPedia Ontology [9] (cross-domain ontology) and others. Most of these vocabularies are structured as general graphs including cycles. Even then most of these vocabularies also include hierarchically organized "is-a" relationships of terms.

In this paper, we focus on taxonomy-based descriptions [10], where a description is seen as a set of terms from a given taxonomy. The creation of such descriptions still remains mostly a manual process, possibly supported by acquisition software (for instance [11]). Usually, such description supports are performed by text analysis techniques (see for instance [12]) and some researches deal with *description propagation* to infer descriptions of derived contents from those of the original contents [13, 14].

The work in [3] which is the basis of our study also proposes a description inference model for composite documents. The description inference model proposed by [3] is mainly intended for document repository management. Based on this model, we proposed a framework for document description authoring, focusing in particular on description creation and description modification [2]. However, our previous work offers no clear discussion of what the requirements for an admissible description should be in order to support an on-line document ecosystem.

This paper is an extension of our previous work and its main goal is to focus on criteria for descriptions to be *admissible*, in the sense that they preserve integrity of document databases and provide enough information to cover document contents.

3   The Model of Composite Documents and Their Descriptions

3.1   Documents and Composite Documents

First of all, our model does *not* consider contents of documents. Our model deals only with structures of document composition and document descriptions. Therefore, we focus only on a document representation consisting of an identifier and a set of *parts*, as this is sufficient for our description management. Therefore, hereafter, when we talk of a document we shall actually mean its representation by an identifier and a set of parts. In order to define a document formally, we assume the existence of a countably infinite set *Doc* whose elements are used by all authors for identifying the created documents. For example, the set *Doc* could be the set of all URIs. In fact, we assume that the creation of a document is tantamount to choosing a (new) element from *Doc* and associating it with a set of other document identifiers that we call its parts.

Definition 1 (The representation of a document). A document consists of an identifier d together with a set of identifiers different than d, called the *parts* of d and denoted as $parts(d)$. If $parts(d) = \emptyset$ then d is called *atomic*, else it is called *composite*.

For notational convenience, we shall often write $d = d_1 + d_2 + \ldots + d_n$ to stand for $parts(d) = \{d_1, d_2, \ldots, d_n\}$.

In this paper, we assume that the structure of every composite document d is a tree in which d is the root, all atomic documents are leaves, and composite documents other than roots are intermediate nodes. Our choice is justified by the fact that (1) the tree is the most suitable structure for representing traditional books that are hierarchically organized, and (2) the tree is also a common structure adopted by many existing document composition environments including open textbook platforms. Based on this assumption, given a composite document d, each part d' of d is called a *child* of d, and d is called the *parent* of d', denoted as $parent(d')$.

It is important to note that in our model the ordering of parts in a composite document is ignored because it is not relevant to our purposes. As we shall see shortly, deriving the description of a composite document from the descriptions of its parts does not depend on any ordering of the parts.

Note that a change in the structure of a composite document may require the use of new identifiers. For example, consider composite document d_0 of Fig. 1 in which the parts d_1, d_2 and d_3 are at the same level. If the author of this composite document decides to group together d_1 and d_2 then it is necessary to introduce a new identifier, say d, to represent this grouping as a composite document. The new structure is shown in Fig. 1.

3.2   Taxonomy-Based Descriptions

Informally, a description in our model is just a set of terms taken from a given taxonomy. We would like to start our explanation about descriptions from the formal definition of taxonomy in our model.

Definition 2 (Taxonomy). Let T be a set of keywords, or *terms*. A *taxonomy* $\mathcal{T}$ defined over T is a pair $(T, \preceq)$ where $\preceq$ is a reflexive and transitive binary relation over T, called *subsumption relation*.

Given two terms, s and t, if $s \preceq t$ then we say that s is *subsumed* by t, or that t *subsumes* s; we also say that s is a *specialization* of t, or that t is a

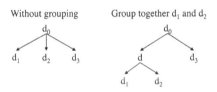

Fig. 1. Grouping of atomic documents

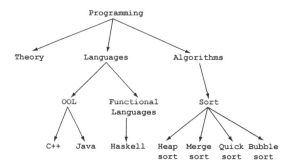

Fig. 2. A taxonomy

generalization of *s*. In our work, we assume that every taxonomy $(T, \preceq)$ is a tree in which the nodes are the terms of T and where there is an arrow $s \rightarrow t$ iff *s* subsumes *t* in $\preceq$. Figure 2 shows the example taxonomy $\mathcal{T}_p$ that we use in this paper. In this example, the term `Sort` subsumes the term `Quick sort`, `OOL` subsumes `Java` and `C++`. Due to the transitivity of the subsumption relation, the term `Programming` subsumes all terms in the tree including itself.

In order to make a document sharable, a description of its content must be provided, so that users can judge whether the document in question matches their needs. Our model allows any set of terms from a taxonomy to be a description.

Definition 3 (Description). Given taxonomy $(T, \preceq)$, we call *description* in T any set of terms from T.

We end this section with an important remark concerning descriptions in general. In reality, a document has several attributes such as author name, title, creation date, and so on. So to describe a document one has to give one value per attribute. Therefore a description of a document should actually be a set of attribute-value pairs. For example the following is a description of a well known book by Agatha Cristie: {(Author, Agatha Cristie), (Title, And then there were none), (Year, 1939), (Content description, novel)}. Note that the description can contain more than one value per attribute (e.g. if the document has more than one author).

The attribute values in such a description usually come from a controlled vocabulary and might be structured in a taxonomy (as is the case for the attribute `Content description` in our example). However, in order to simplify the presentation, we have assumed only one attribute for describing documents in this paper, namely `Content description`. As a consequence, we omit the attribute name in the description of a document and give only the set of attribute values. Moreover we have assumed that the values of this unique attribute are organized in a taxonomy.

Extending our results to descriptions involving more than one attribute is rather straightforward: instead of having single attribute values we will have tuples of values, and what needs to be done then is to define a subsumption relation over tuples based on the subsumption relations over the individual attribute values. This extension lies outside the scope of the present paper and will be reported in future work.

As a final remark, note that the definition of a description as a set of attribute-value pairs can be represented in RDF in a straightforward way. Indeed, each pair {(`Attr`, `Value`)} can be represented by the RDF triple {$(d$, `Attr`, `Value`)}, where d is the identifier of the document being described. This means that the document repository can then use the powerful reasoning system of RDF in order to handle description inferences; and moreover, the document repository can then communicate with other repositories using RDF, and in particular it can communicate with the world wide web. Similar advantages can be obtained using any other standard vocabulary of the Linked Open World (LOD). Indeed, the framework that we propose here works with any kind of controlled vocabulary. In fact, this ease to map to widely-used controlled vocabularies, gives a document repository based on our model enhanced visibility, searchability, and reusability of documents in the context of the world-wide-web. In a nutshell, descriptions in our model are easy to define and easy to map to RDF (with all the advantages entailed by such a mapping).

3.3   Inferred Descriptions

Reduction of a Description. A description can be redundant if some of its terms are subsumed by other terms in the description. For instance, the description {`Sorting`, `Quick sort`, `java`} is redundant, as `Sorting` subsumes `Quick sort`. Redundant descriptions are sometimes undesirable as they can lead to redundant computations. Therefore we introduce the concept of non-redundant, or *reduced description*, defined as follows:

Definition 4 (Reduced description). Given taxonomy $(T, \preceq)$, a set of terms D from T is called *reduced* if for any terms s and t in D, $s \not\preceq t$ and $t \not\preceq s$.

In general, from the same redundant description we can derive multiple no-redundant descriptions, by either keeping only its maximal terms, or by keeping only its minimal terms. In this paper we consider both types of non redundant descriptions. Hence the following definitions:

Definition 5 (Cover of a description). Let D be a description in taxonomy $(T, \preceq)$. we call *cover* of D, denoted as $cover(D)$, the set of maximal terms in D.

Definition 6 (Reduction of a description). Let D be a description in taxonomy $(T, \preceq)$. we call *reduction* of D, denoted as $red(D)$, the set of minimal terms in D.

In our previous example, where $D = \{$`Sorting`, `Quicksort`, `java`$\}$, we have: $cover(D) = \{$`Sorting`, `java`$\}$ and $red(D) = \{$`Quicksort`, `java`$\}$. Note that every term in D is subsumed by some term in the cover and that every term in the cover subsumes some term in D.

Algorithm cover

> *Input* a description D
> *Output* $cover(D)$
>
> $C \leftarrow \emptyset$
> **for all** $t \in D$ **do**
>   **if** there is no $t' \in D$ such that $t' \succ t$ **then**
> $C \leftarrow C \cup \{t\}$
>   **end if**
> **end for**
> **return** C

Algorithm reduction

> *Input* a description D
> *Output* $red(D)$
>
> $R \leftarrow \emptyset$
> **for all** $t \in D$ **do**
>   **if** there is no $t' \in D$ such that $t' \prec t$ **then**
> $R \leftarrow R \cup \{t\}$
>   **end if**
> **end for**
> **return** R

Algorithm summary

> *Input* a document d
> *Output* $summary(d)$
>
> **if** d is atomic **then**
>   **return** $cover(ADescr(d))$
> **end if**
> **for all** $d_i \in parts(d), i = 1, \ldots, n$ **do**
> $D_i \leftarrow$ summary(d_i)
> **end for**
> $P \leftarrow D_1 \times D_2 \times \ldots \times D_n$
> **for all** $L_k = [t_1^k, \ldots, t_n^k] \in P, k = 1, .., l$ **do**
> $T_k \leftarrow lub_{\preceq}(t_1^k, \ldots, t_n^k)$
> **end for**
> **return** $red(T_1, \ldots, T_l)$

$lub_{\preceq}(t_1, \ldots, t_n)$ returns the least upper bound of the set of terms $t_1, \ldots, t_n$ with respect to $\preceq$.

Fig. 3. cover, reduction and summary algorithm

Also note that every term in the description subsumes a term in the reduction, and there is no term in the reduction that is NOT subsumed by a term in the description. In other words, the reduction is the most compact and accurate representation of a redundant description, for searching purposes. For example, if a user wants to find documents describing something related to sorting, in the above example we can find the term Sorting in both, the $cover(D)$ and the reduction $red(D)$. But if a user wants to find documents related to "Quick sort", the term Quick sort appears only in $red(D)$ and not in $cover(D)$. So $red(D)$ keeps more accurate terms from the original redundant description than $cover(D)$ does. Therefore $red(d)$ is more accurate than $cover(D)$.

The algorithms for computing the cover and the reduction of a description are illustrated in Fig. 3.

We note here that the cover, as well as other related concepts that we shall introduce shortly are used only internally to generate all admissible descriptions. It is up to the author to choose one among the admissible descriptions proposed by the authoring system. The chosen description then becomes *the* document description, and it is stored (along with the document identifier) in the document repository.

Based on the concepts of reduction and cover of a description, we now define some additional concepts to be used in the definition of admissible description.

Cover of a Document. Intuitively, the description of a composite document must incorporate somehow the descriptions of the document's parts (and therefore, recursively, the descriptions of the document's components). To state this intuition formally, we have to extend the concept of cover from a single description to a set of descriptions.

Definition 7 (Cover of a document). Let $d = d_1 + \ldots + d_n$, be a document with part descriptions $D_1, \ldots, D_n$, respectively. The *cover* of d, denoted as $cover(d)$, is a description defined as $cover(d) = cover(D_1 \cup \ldots \cup D_n)$.

For example, if d has two parts with descriptions $D_1 = \{$Sorting, Quick sort, java$\}$ and $D_2 = \{$Bubble sort, C++$\}$ then $cover(d) = \{$Sorting, java, C++$\}$. Note that the description obtained by simply taking the union of D_1 and D_2 gives an accurate but redundant description of the contents of the composite document.

Summary of a Document. Sometimes we want to summarize the topics contained in a big composite document. There are several possible approaches for summarization, and one of them is to use the document cover. Another approach is to extract common topics shared by all components of the document. For example, consider a composite document $d = d_1 + d_2$ with $\{d_1\} = \{$Quick sort, Java$\}$ and $\{d_2\} = \{$Bubble sort, C++$\}$. In this case, the description $D_{sum} = \{$Sort, OOL$\}$ is a possible summary of d_1 and d_2. Indeed, Sort subsumes both Quick sort and Bubble sort, and OOL also subsumes both Java and C++. Therefore $\{$Sort, OOL$\}$ represents what d_1 and d_2 have in common.

In this example, $D'_{sum} = \{$Algorithms, Languages$\}$ is also a possible summary. However, D'_{sum} is less accurate than D_{sum}. The most extreme example is $D^*_{sum} = \{$Programming$\}$. D^*_{sum} summarizes any description in T but with the lowest accuracy. Usually such an over-general summary is useless for document search.

Now, intuitively, we can define the *summary of a document* as a description which (a) summarizes what all components of the document have in common in their descriptions and (b) it is minimal, in other words, has highest accuracy. The descriptions D'_{sum} and D^*_{sum} violate the second criterion because they have lower accuracy than D_{sum}.

In order to state this intuition formally, we introduce the following refinement relation over reduced descriptions.

Definition 8 (Refinement relation). Let D_1 and D_2 be two descriptions. We say that D_1 is *finer* than D_2, denoted $D_1 \sqsubseteq D_2$, iff $\forall t_2 \in D_2, \exists t_1 \in D_1 \wedge t_1 \preceq t_2$.

For example, D_{sum} is finer than D'_{sum}, as for every term t in D'_{sum}, we can find a term in D_{sum} subsumed by t. Indeed, Sort $\preceq$ Algorithms and OOL $\preceq$ Languages.

The refinement relation $\sqsubseteq$ is clearly reflexive and transitive. Moreover, over reduced descriptions, $\sqsubseteq$ becomes antisymmetric. From these properties we can say that $\sqsubseteq$ is a partial order over reduced descriptions (see [3] for more details). The following proposition states a more general property of the partial order $\sqsubseteq$, namely that it is a complete lattice. It is in this lattice that the summary of a composite document can be defined formally.

Proposition 1. The set of all reduced descriptions forms a complete lattice U under the ordering $\sqsubseteq$. Moreover, for given a set $D = \{D_1, \ldots, D_n\}$ of reduced descriptions, U has least upper bound (lub), denoted as $lub(\mathcal{D}, \sqsubseteq)$ and greatest lower bound (glb), denoted as $glb(\mathcal{D}, \sqsubseteq)$.

The least upper bound of a set of descriptions is the most accurate set of terms representing what the descriptions have in common. Therefore, by obtaining the *lub* of descriptions of documents, we can get the most accurate description that summarizes what the documents have in common. By using this proposition, we can now define the summary of a document as follows:

Definition 9 (Summary of a document). Given a document d, the *summary* of d, denoted as $sum(d)$, is a description defined as follows:

- if d is atomic, $sum(d) = cover(D)$,
- else, for $d = d_1 + \ldots + d_n$, let $\mathcal{D} = \{sum(d_1), \ldots, sum(d_n)\}$, $sum(d) = lub(\mathcal{D}, \sqsubseteq)$.

The algorithm `summary` illustrated in Fig. 3 recursively computes the summary of a given document.

4   Admissible Descriptions

In this section, we would like to explain how we can use inferred descriptions of documents to help users to create and manage document descriptions. As we already mentioned, the author description of a document is left entirely up to description authors. Therefore, the algorithms explained in the previous section are not intended to *generate* descriptions of documents automatically. The role of the algorithms is to *suggest* inferred descriptions to avoid making descriptions from scratch. Before describing the principles underlying our suggestion process, we would like to introduce a basic concept, namely that of admissible description.

Admissible Descriptions. In order to define the concept of admissible description, the basic question is the following: are there any conditions that descriptions should satisfy in order to be admissible?

To begin with, intuitively, the description of a document should not be more general than the summary of the document. Consider for example a document d with two parts having the following descriptions: $D_1 = \{$Quick sort, Java$\}$, $D_2 = \{$Bubble sort, C++$\}$. The summary of d is then the following description: $Sum(d) = \{$Sorting, OOL$\}$ The description $\{$Computer Science$\}$ strictly subsumes the summary of d and is therefore too general to describe d. On the other hand, the descriptions $\{$Sorting, Java, C++$\}$ and $\{$Quick sort, Bubble sort, OOL$\}$ are both subsumed by the summary of d and therefore each of them can be used to describe d (and so can the summary itself).

Note that none of these two descriptions is better than the other (in fact they are not comparable); the description $\{$Sorting, Java, C++$\}$ would be used if the author wanted to emphasize the language aspect of the content of d, while the description {Quick sort, Bubble sort, OOL} would be used if the author wanted to emphasize the algorithmic aspect of the content of d.

However for a description to be *admissible*, it is not sufficient to just be subsumed by the summary of the document being described. Suppose for example that the descriptions of the two parts of d were the following: $D_1 =$ {Quick sort, Java}, $D_2 =$ {Bubble sort, C++, Analytics}. Then the summary remains the same: $Sum(d) =$ {Sorting, OOL}. Consider now the following description: $D =$ {Quick sort, Java, Bubble sort, C++}. This description is subsumed by the summary, yet it leaves out the term Analytics (i.e. it does not subsume the cover of d). On the other hand, if we remove the term Analytics from D_2 and add it to D then D is still subsumed by the summary but the term Analytics in description D of d does not appear in the descriptions of the components of d. In other words, D is simply a "bad" description because it describes something which does not appear in the descriptions of its parts.

To summarize our discussion so far, a description D should be subsumed by the summary, and moreover it should be *sound* and *complete* in order to be admissible. By soundness we mean that each term of D should subsume some term of the cover; and by completeness we mean that each term in the cover should be subsumed by some term of D. These requirements are stated formally in the following definition.

Definition 10 (Admissible description). *Let Cover(d) and Sum(d) be the cover and the summary of a document d. A reduced description D is called an admissible description of d if the following conditions hold:*

- *$D \sqsubseteq Sum(d)$*
- *for each term t in D there is a term s in cover(d) such that $s \preceq t$ (soundness)*
- *for each term s in cover(d) there is a term t in D such that $s \preceq t$ (completeness)*

Soundness of descriptions is an indispensable property for every description in order to preserve integrity of document databases. If a description of a composite document doesn't satisfy soundness, it means that the description contains a term which is not in the description of any component of the document. Documents with non-sound descriptions may appear as non-relevant documents in document search results.

On the other hand, completeness comes from a more practical requirement, namely the requirement of "minimal surprise". Intuitively, this requirement is satisfied if every term in a component description or a generalization thereof appears in the description of its parent. This constraint minimizes the risk that a reader meets unexpected contents in a document (i.e. contents not mentioned in the document description).

Note that the cover is always an admissible description. The summary on the other hand is not always an admissible description, though it is always a sound description.

Clearly, in a composite document with a big number of components the number of admissible descriptions might be quite large, and choosing one among many admissible descriptions becomes a rather tedious task. Hence the need for a user friendly interface helping the user to choose, in a systematic manner, one among possibly many admissible descriptions. In the remaining of this section we outline some basic principles that such an *authoring system* should follow.

The scenario that we consider is that of an author composing a document and having at least a fair knowledge of the subject area of the documents being composed (e.g. computer science, literature etc.) as well as of the taxonomy being used. The author has two options: either to ask the authoring system to suggest an admissible description for the composite document or to submit his own description to the authoring system for approval. In both cases the authoring system uses the inference mechanisms that we saw earlier in order to generate admissible descriptions or to check proposed descriptions for admissibility.

In the first case, the authoring system will generate all admissible descriptions of the composite document and will present them to the author so that he can choose one. In the second case, the authoring system will check whether the description proposed by the author is an admissible description; if yes, then the description is accepted, otherwise an interaction takes place between the author and the authoring system. During this interaction, the authoring system helps the author to modify his description so that it becomes admissible.

If the proposed description is found to be non-admissible, this means that it does not satisfy soundness or completeness. To see what kind of interaction is taking place in this case, let $ADescr(d)$ denote the description proposed by the author for a composite document d, and suppose that $d = d_1 + d_2$. Moreover, suppose that $ADescr(d_1)=$ {Quick sort, Java}, $ADescr(d_2) =$ {Bubble sort, C++} and $ADescr(d) =$ {Sort, Theory}. This description does not satisfy soundness because none of the terms in d_1 and d_2 is subsumed by Theory in $ADescr(d)$. In this case, the authoring system can suggest the following two options:

– Remove terms: the system suggests to remove Theory from $ADescr(d)$.
– Add components: the system shows to the user a list of components whose descriptions contain a term $t \preceq$ Theory and suggests the addition of one of them.

On the other hand, if a description does not satisfy completeness, then the system can again suggest two options. For example, the author description $ADescr(d) =$ {Bubble sort, OOL}, does not satisfy completeness due to lack of mention about Quick sort in $ADescr(d_1)$. A reader who intends to learn about bubble sort may be surprised when he faces a description of quick sort which is not mentioned in the description. In this case, the author has the following two options:

– Remove components: the system suggests to remove d_1 from the composite document.

– Add or generalize terms: the system shows a list of terms $\{t\}$ satisfying $t \succeq$ `Quicksort` and suggests the addition of one of them, or generalizes a term in $ADescr(d)$ by one of them. For instance, an author can add `Quick sort` to $ADescr(d)$, or replace `Bubble sort` in $ADescr(d)$ by `Sort` which subsumes both `Quick sort` and `Bubble sort`.

Such a description improvement process is usually an interactive process because modification of a description in order to satisfy one property may break another property. For each modification made by authors the authoring system should check soundness and completeness and suggest next options if a modified description does not satisfy these properties.

5   Concluding Remarks

We have seen a method for describing composite documents based on the descriptions of their components. We defined an ordering on reduced descriptions and gave algorithms for inferring descriptions based on that ordering. We also used the description ordering to introduce the concept of "admissible description"; and argued that admissible descriptions are the most appropriate for composite documents. However, as the number of such descriptions might be large, we discussed an interactive approach allowing authors of composite documents to build descriptions incrementally with the help of an authoring system.

The important features of descriptions as defined in this paper is that they are easy to use and easy to map to RDF. This means that document repositories based on our model have enhanced visibility, searchability, and reusability of their documents in the context of the world wide web.

Our current work focuses on two topics:

– The extension of the model to handle descriptions over two or more attributes (not just over the attribute Content Description). As we mentioned in the paper, such an extension is possible and involves mainly the extension of the ordering from descriptions over the values of a single attribute to descriptions over tuples of values defined on two or more attributes.
– The design of an authoring system using the basic principles discussed in the paper.

References

1. Connexions web site. http://cnx.org/
2. Sugibuchi, T., Tuan, L.A., Spyratos, N.: Metadata inference for description authoring in a document composition environment. In: Agosti, M., Esposito, F., Ferilli, S., Ferro, N. (eds.) IRCDL 2012. CCIS, vol. 354, pp. 69–80. Springer, Heidelberg (2013)
3. Rigaux, P., Spyratos, N.: Metadata inference for document retrieval in a distributed repository. In: Maher, M.J. (ed.) ASIAN 2004. LNCS, vol. 3321, pp. 418–436. Springer, Heidelberg (2004)

4. OWL 2 Web Ontology Language Document Overview. http://www.w3.org/TR/owl2-overview/
5. SKOS Simple Knowledge Organization System Reference. http://www.w3.org/TR/skos-reference/
6. Coulter, N.: ACM's computing classification system reflects changing times. Commun. ACM **40**(12), 111–112 (1997)
7. The Gene Ontology Consortium. Gene ontology: tool for the unification of biology. Nat. Genet. **25**(1), 25–29 (2000)
8. AAT Web site. http://www.getty.edu/research/tools/vocabularies/aat/
9. The DBPedia Ontology. http://wiki.dbpedia.org/Ontology
10. Baeza-Yates, R., Ribeiro-Neto, B. (eds.): Modern Information Retrieval. Addison-Wesley, Boston (1999)
11. Erdmann, M., Maedche, A., Schnurr, H.-P., Staab, S.: From manual to semi-automatic semantic annotation: about ontology-based text annotation tools. In: Proceedings of the COLING International Workshop on Semantic Annotation and Intelligent Context (2000)
12. Handschuh, S., Staab, S., Volz, R.: On deep annotation. In: Proceedings of International World Wide Web Conference (WWW), pp. 431–438 (2003)
13. Pastorello Jr, G.Z., Daltio, J., Medeiros, C.B.: Multimedia semantic annotation propagation. In: Proceedings of IEEE International Symposium on Multimedia (ISM) 08, pp. 509–514 (2008)
14. Leung, M.-K., Mandl, T., Lee, E.A., Latronico, E., Shelton, C., Tripakis, S., Lickly, B.: Scalable semantic annotation using lattice-based ontologies. In: Schürr, A., Selic, B. (eds.) MODELS 2009. LNCS, vol. 5795, pp. 393–407. Springer, Heidelberg (2009)

Rewriting Aggregate Queries Using Functional Dependencies within the Cloud

Romain Perriot[1]([✉]), Laurent d'Orazio[1], Dominique Laurent[2],
and Nicolas Spyratos[3]

[1] LIMOS UMR 6158, Clermont Université, CNRS, Université Blaise Pascal,
Clermont-Ferrand, France
{romain.perriot,laurent.dorazio}@univ-bpclermont.fr
[2] ETIS UMR 8051, ENSEA, CNRS, Universite de Cergy Pontoise,
Cergy-Pontoise, France
dominique.laurent@u-cergy.fr
[3] LRI UMR 8623, UniverSud Paris, CNRS, Université Paris Sud, Orsay, France
nicolas.spyratos@lri.fr

Abstract. Since many years, companies and laboratories have had a pressing need for processing large amounts of data in areas such as astronomy, medicine or social networks. Cloud computing provides users with a virtually infinite amount of computing resources. Scaling up cloud performance can be usually achieved by using more numerous and/or more powerful nodes. However, this results in high costs as well as using more resources than necessary. In the area of databases, caching and query rewriting are two important ways to improve performance. This paper proposes rewriting rules for aggregate queries using semantic caching in the cloud. We have implemented our proposal in the Pig system and conducted experiments in a private cloud.

Keywords: Databases · Data warehouses · Optimization · Rewriting · Cloud computing · Caching

1 Introduction

Cloud computing [5] aims to tackle increasing needs of computing and storage resources, enabling to envision data management at an unexpected scale in various contexts (medical imagery, particles physics, cultural heritage). As a consequence, it has attracted an increasing interest, in particular by major IT companies such as Google, Microsoft, Amazon, Yahoo! or Facebook. These providers offer different data management systems in the cloud using various pricing models, like large scale systems with a simplified query interface (like Amazon SimpleDB [3] or DynamoDB [1]), or fully relational but less scalable systems (such as Amazon RDS [2] and SQL Azure [19]). In addition, several data intensive analysis tools have been proposed, such as Pig [20], Hive [23], SCOPE [7] or Jaql [6] differing in their data model and querying language.

A. Kawtrakul et al. (Eds.): ISIP 2013, CCIS 421, pp. 31–42, 2014.
DOI: 10.1007/978-3-319-08732-0_3, © Springer International Publishing Switzerland 2014

Performance of these systems usually relies on brute force (i.e. using more numerous and/or more powerful nodes) resulting in high cost and suboptimal resource management. Performance optimization in databases has been studied for years, in particular using methods such as indexing, materialized views, prefetching or caching. These methods would help improve the performance in the cloud, optimizing resource management. In particular, semantic caches [10,16] enable to rewrite queries so as to reuse local results from previous requests. Nevertheless, a cache is efficient only if it is tuned for a given context. The combination of various data management systems and pricing models lead to a major challenge: how to select relevant caching strategies according to a given provider, a specific data management system and a set of constraints on performance and/or budget.

Some recent approaches [11,15,24] address part of the problem, considering data sharing and optimization with respect to the pay-as-you-go model. These solutions are quite orthogonal to ours, since we consider a specific type of caching, namely semantic caching, studying in detail the query evaluation process. In previous work, we have proposed CoopSC [25] consisting of a semantic cache relying on a P2P system; our preliminary experiments on CoopSC in the cloud highlighted potential savings. However, CoopSC caching strategies do not consider elasticity of the cloud with regard to the budget, nor do they take into consideration the data model or language of the different systems. Recently, rewriting rules were integrated in SCOPE, so as to consider common subexpressions [22]. Nevertheless, this approach is system dependent and does not take into account monetary aspects.

In this paper, we address the problem of optimizing performance in massive data analysis systems. To achieve this goal, our main contributions are (1) rewriting rules for maximizing a cache utility for OLAP and (2) cache management policies for query processing and replacement. Our approach is then validated for massive data analysis in a private cloud, using the Pig system. This article extends our previous contribution [17] in three ways: (i) it details the cache management based on the rewriting rules, (ii) it fully integrates the approach in a cloud data analysis system, namely Pig and (iii) it presents experimental results.

The remainder of this paper is organized as follows. In Sect. 2, we present the rewriting rules and Sect. 3 details the management strategy of our cache. In Sect. 4, we present experimental results of our approach in a cloud environment, and in Sect. 5, we discuss the state of the art and compare it to our approach. In Sect. 6, we conclude the paper.

2   Aggregate Query Rewriting Rules

We define an OLAP query as the agregation over the attribute set X of a measure attribute M using an aggregate function $aggr$. In SQL, the query can be written as follow:

SELECT X, $aggr(M)$ AS result

FROM T

GROUP BY X

T is the fact table with all the needed joins with the dimension tables. In this work, we consider that only the attribute set X and the aggregate function $aggr$ are variable. From this and for the rest of the paper, we use the notation $Q = \langle X, aggr \rangle$ to describe a query Q which is the aggregation over the attribute set X of the measure attribute M using the aggregate function $aggr$.

2.1   Partition and Query Comparison

An aggregate query $Q = \langle X, aggr \rangle$ generates a partition $\Pi(Q)$ which is based on the values of the attribute set X. Given two queries $Q_1 = \langle X_1, aggr_1 \rangle$, $Q_2 = \langle X_2, aggr_2 \rangle$ and their associated partitions $\Pi(Q_1)$ and $\Pi(Q_2)$, if each block of $\Pi(Q_1)$ (i.e. each group of Q_1) is in a unique block of $\Pi(Q_2)$ (i.e. each group of Q_2) (which is $\Pi(Q_1) \sqsubseteq \Pi(Q_2)$ holds), then it is possible to group the blocks from $\Pi(Q_1)$ to obtain $\Pi(Q_2)$. Assuming we have sufficient informations associated to each group of Q_1, it is possible to compute the result of Q_2 from the result of Q_1. From that, we define the pre-ordering binary operatory (i.e. reflexive and transitive) $\preceq$ ("less") that is $Q_1 \preceq Q_2$ holds if and only if $\Pi(Q_1) \sqsubseteq \Pi(Q_2)$ holds. Because of the properties of this operator, we also define the operator $\equiv$ that is $Q_1 \equiv Q_2$ holds if and only if $Q_1 \preceq Q_2$ and $Q_2 \preceq Q_1$ hold. About the partitions, $Q_1 \equiv Q_2$ holds if and only if $\Pi(Q_1) = \Pi(Q_2)$ holds. We finally define the operator $\prec$ ("strictly less") that is $Q_1 \prec Q_2$ holds if and only if $Q_1 \preceq Q_2$ holds and $Q_1 \equiv Q_2$ does not hold.

From the SQL GROUP BY operator, we can easily see that if $X_2 \subseteq X_1$ holds then $Q_1 \preceq Q_2$ holds. Let X_i^+ be the closure of X_i using the set of functional dependencies and the queries $Q_1 = \langle X_1, aggr_1 \rangle$ and $Q_1^+ = \langle X_1^+, aggr_1 \rangle$; it is important to notice that $\Pi(Q_1) = \Pi(Q_1^+)$ holds which is that grouping by X_1^+ will generate the same partition as grouping by X_1: we have $Q_1 \equiv Q_1^+$. From this remark, if $X_2 \subseteq X_1^+$ (or $X_2^+ \subseteq X_1^+$) holds then $Q_1 \preceq Q_2$ holds, if $X_2^+ = X_1^+$ holds then $Q_1 \equiv Q_2$ holds and if $X_2^+ \subset X_1^+$ holds then $Q_1 \prec Q_2$ holds. It is possible to compare the attribute sets (or their closure) X_1 and X_2 to compare the queries Q_1 and Q_2.

2.2   Aggregate Function

In this work, we consider the aggregate functions min, max, sum, $count$ and avg. An aggregate function $aggr$ is associative if for every partition $\Pi(R)$ of the relation R, we have the following property:

$$aggr(R) = aggr(\{aggr(P) \mid P \in \Pi(R)\})$$

This property describes the fact that we can compute the aggregation of the entire relation by aggregating the results of the pre-aggregation using the same function. The aggregate functions *min*, *max* and *sum* are associatives. For the aggregate functions *count* and *avg*, we have the following specific properties:

$$count(R) = sum(\{count(P) \mid P \in \Pi(R)\})$$
$$avg(R) = sum(R)/count(R)$$
$$avg(R) = \frac{sum(\{sum(P) \mid P \in \Pi(R)\})}{sum(\{count(P) \mid P \in \Pi(R)\})}$$

Let Q_i^* be $Q_i^* = \langle X_i^+,\ min,\ max,\ sum,\ count \rangle$ which is in SQL format:

SELECT X_i^+, $min(M)$ AS min_Q, $max(M)$ AS max_Q,

                    $sum(M)$ AS sum_Q, $count(M)$ AS $count_Q$

FROM T

GROUP BY X_i^+

and $Q_i(\Delta)$ the result of the query Q_i on the database instance Δ, if we have $Q_1^* \preceq Q_2$, we can compute $Q_2(\Delta)$ using $Q_1^*(\Delta)$. We define $expr_0$ and $expr_1$ as follow:

$$expr_0(aggr) = \begin{cases} aggr_Q & \text{if } aggr \text{ is associative} \\ count_Q & \text{if } aggr = count \\ sum_Q/count_Q & \text{if } aggr = avg \end{cases}$$

$$expr_1(aggr) = \begin{cases} aggr(aggr_Q) & \text{if } aggr \text{ is associative} \\ sum(count_Q) & \text{if } aggr = count \\ \frac{sum(sum_Q)}{sum(count_Q)} & \text{if } aggr = avg \end{cases}$$

There is two cases for rewriting Q_2 from $Q_1^*(\Delta)$.

- If $Q_1^* \equiv Q_2$ holds then we just have to do the projection over the attribute set X_2 on $Q_1^*(\Delta)$ and generate $expr_0(aggr_2)$. In SQL, we will have:

    SELECT X_2, $expr_0(aggr_2)$ AS result
    FROM $Q_1^*(\Delta)$

- If $Q_1^* \prec Q_2$ holds then we can rewrite Q_2 as $Q_2 = \langle X_2,\ expr_1(aggr_2) \rangle (Q_1^*\Delta)$. In SQL, we will have:

    SELECT X_2, $expr_1(aggr_2)$ AS result
    FROM $Q_1^*(\Delta)$
    GROUP BY X_2

The fact that Q_1^* groups by X_1^+ and generates the results of the aggregation of the functions *min*, *max*, *sum* and *count* allows more queries to be rewritten using $Q_1^*(\Delta)$. Because $Q_1 \equiv Q_1^*$, it is possible to rewrite Q_1 to Q_1^* in order to use $Q_1^*(\Delta)$ for rewriting future incoming queries. For the incoming query Q_2, the rewriting rule we propose is to systematiquely rewrite Q_2 to use $Q_1^*(\Delta)$ if such a result exists and $Q_1^* \preceq Q_2$ holds.

3   Cache Management

We propose a cache management policy (described in the Algorithm 1, with an incoming query Q) that uses the rewriting rules we have defined.

> **Input**: Q
> $Q_i \leftarrow lookup(Q)$;
> if Q_i *not exists* **then**
> | Compute Q^*;
> | bind(Q^*);
> | $Q_i \leftarrow Q^*$;
> **end**
> Compute Q from Q_i;

Algorithm 1. Cache management algorithm

"Lookup" is the action to research a usable Q_i from the cache such that $Q_i \preceq Q$. "Bind" add the result of the query to the cache and remove all entries Q_i from the cache where $Q^* \preceq Q_i$. We can notice that several queries can be candidate to be used for resolving an incoming query; a user defined strategy is used to choose the best one. Such strategies are to choose the entry with less bytes stored, less tuples or using statistics associated to entries to estimate the execution time.

Our storing strategy keeps in cache only entries that do not overlap which is an effective way to optimize cache content.

We consider that our cache is a semantic cache because it is working about the meaning of its entries. Our proposition differs from [10] which propose semantic caching based on selecting predicates which is orthogonal to our proposition: they consider selections when we consider aggregations. An other important thing to notice is that our queries are not splitted into a probe query and a remainder query because if we use a cache entry, we only retrieve the data from it without using other data. Finally, this cache management strategy does not take into account the available storage space for selecting entries to remove. In addition to our cache content policy, the user can choose a replacement policy to remove some entries when there is not enough space or increase automatically cloud resources.

4   Experiments

4.1   Experimental Setup

The experiments were conducted on a virtual cluster composed of 20 virtual machines with a 8 GB disk, 2 GB of RAM and 1 vCPU. The physical architecture consisting of four quadri-pros 2.1 GHz with 96 GB of RAM. All machines feature Hadoop (version 0.20.2 with a 64 Mb chunck size and 2 copies) [4] and Pig Latin (version 0.11.1) [20].

In order to validate our solution we choose the dataset of the well known and approved Star Schema Benchmark [21] (more precisely SSB 2.1.8.18) with a scale factor of 10 (which is about 6 GB). A cache using this query rewriting and management strategy has been developed in C++11.

In our experiments, we mainly focus on the *customer* dimension (27 MB for 300 K customers) which is composed of eight attributes in two hierarchies and the measure attribute *lo_revenue* in the *lineorder* fact table. Four attributes are equivalent which is that for two attributes A and B, the two functional dependencies $A \rightarrow B$ and $B \rightarrow A$ hold (we note $A \leftrightarrow B$). This four attributes are *c_custkey*, *c_name*, *c_address* and *c_phone* (A customer identified by a unique key has a unique name, a unique phone number and lives at a unique address). The market segment hierarchy is *c_name* $\rightarrow$ *c_mktsegment* (a customer belongs to only one market segment) while the geography hierarchy is *c_address* $\rightarrow$ *c_city* $\rightarrow$ *c_nation* $\rightarrow$ *c_region* (an address is in a city which is in a nation which is in a world region). We notice that the four equivalent attributes are at the root (most detailed) of the two hierarchies; extending one of this attributes among the functional dependencies will produce the schema of the entire *customer* dimension.

4.2   Experimental Results

The query rewriting which occurs when there is a cache miss extends the attribute set and adds more aggregation results. Because there is more attributes in the result set, the system has to manage more bytes which is a very important bottleneck in MapReduce paradigm since data has to be shuffle between Map and Reduce phases; Fig. 1 shows that point. For each group, four aggregation are computed which can also increase the execution time, Fig. 1 shows that what and how many aggregation functions we compute seems to be trifling. In our implementation using Pig Latin, the result of the incoming query (with a cache miss) Q is not computed at the same time as Q^* but is computed after. This involves to an

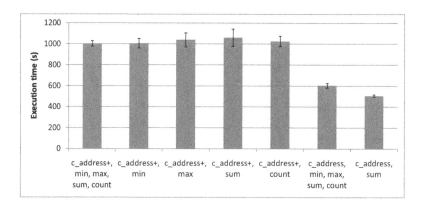

Fig. 1. Execution time of Group By Pig Latin queries

other MapReduce job to be launched and to increase the execution time. In our implementation, the comparisons to create groups are computed over X^+ and not simply over X which increase the execution time; custom MapReduce programs could take care about this issue.

Roll-up and Drill-down are two OLAP operators which give results more aggregated and more detailed respectively. Within the *customer* geography hierarchy, Roll-up is to compute aggregations from *c_address* to *c_region* and Drill-down to compute aggregations from *c_region* to *c_address*. Because of the cache management policy which behaves to evolve to keep the most detailed queries, a Drill-down will do a cache miss each time while a Roll-up will always reuse the first computed cache entry. In Fig. 2, we can see that a drill-down is very expensive. In the other hand, Fig. 3 shows that our cache management policy is very effective in case of roll-up.

Processing $\langle c\_address^+, aggr \rangle$ is (very) expensive (as shown in Fig. 1) because all the eight attributes are keeped which is expensive in MapReduce paradigm but keeping these eight attributes allows more queries to be rewritten, decreasing their

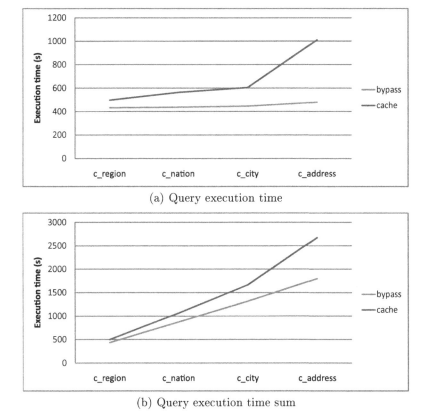

(a) Query execution time

(b) Query execution time sum

Fig. 2. Drill-down execution time

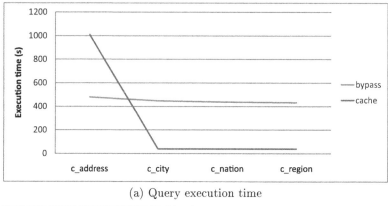

(a) Query execution time

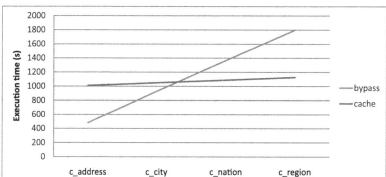

(b) Query execution time sum

Fig. 3. Roll-up execution time

processing time from -90% to -95%. Taking only into account the *customer* dimension, all the 1280 (2^8 attribute sets and 5 aggregate functions) possible GROUP BY queries can be rewritten using $\langle c\_address^+, aggr \rangle$, no matter what aggregation function $aggr$ is. Figure 4(a) shows different execution time from cache (and what cache entry was used) or when a cache miss occurs. We can see (from Figs. 4(a) and 5(a)) that computing a query from the cache takes few time compared to computing it directly. In Figs. 4(b) and 5(b), we can see that the overload of the cache miss is amortized the first time the cache entry is reused in almost all cases.

5   Related Work

5.1   Rewriting

The problem of optimizing semantically related queries has received a lot of attention during the last decades. Main references are presented into a wide survey on this topic [14].

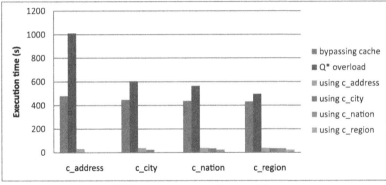

(a) Execution time from cache

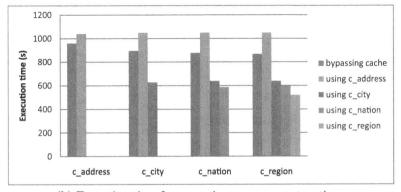

(b) Execution time for executing same query two times

Fig. 4. Execution time from cache

Our approach differs from these solutions in a main way. To the best of our knowledge, it is the first approach to OLAP query rewriting in which the content of the cache is optimized which is, our content management strategy automatically deletes entries which are overlapped by others without reducing the set of queries that can be answered by the cache alone. This differs from usual replacement policies such as LRU which reduce that set.

5.2 Semantic Caching

Semantic caching has been studied in several contexts: distributed databases [10,16], web [8,9,18] and grid computing [13]. These solutions differ in several ways. The cache can thus store query results [10] called *semantic regions* or *semantic segments*, objects to be strongly [16] or independently [13] associated to and possibly shared by predicates. Some of them focus on a specific data structure like XML [8,18]. Efficient research, via *signature files* has been proposed for keyword based and conjunctive queries. In a previous work, we deployed P2P

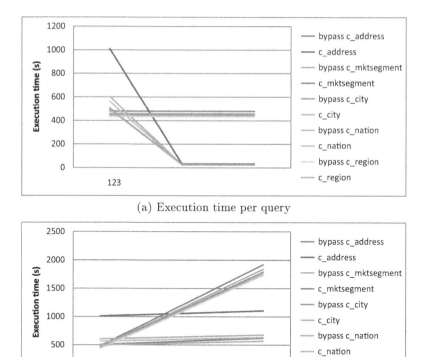

(a) Execution time per query

(b) Execution time sum

Fig. 5. Execution time iterated

semantic caches, called CoopSC [25] to highlight potential money savings in the cloud, in addition to traditional time and bandwidth consumption reductions.

All these techniques are complementary to our project and can be reused to provide finely tuned caches.

5.3 Data Management in the Cloud

Data management in the cloud has attracted a lot of attention during the last years. Major IT companies like Amazon, Facebook, Google, IBM, Microsoft or Yahoo! have provided large scale data management systems. Some of them consists on large scale solutions providing a simplified query interface (usually a subset of SQL), like Amazon SimpleDB [3] or DynamoDB [1]. Less scalable but fully relational approach are also available, such as Amazon RDS [2] and SQL Azure [19]. Data intensive analysis tools such as Pig [20], Hive [23], SCOPE [7] or Jaql [6], relying on massively parallel execution environment like MapReduce [12], or its open source version Hadoop [4] have been developed.

To the best of our knowledge, caching has not been intensively addressed in these systems (even if some works start to consider reusing common subexpressions for query processing [22]).

6   Conclusion

In this position paper, we presented a rewriting technique for aggregate queries in the context of data-warehouses. We then propose a cache solution relying on these rewriting rules to process queries and manage, especially replace, the cache entries. The solution has been validated experimentally in the context of data analysis in the cloud using the Pig system.

Many perspectives are opened by this research. We would like to validate our solution in different systems (Hive, Jaql or MonetDB) and contexts. In particular, we are interested in applying such an approach in a e-learning environment on cloud computing, as part of the GOD project (http://home.isima.fr/god/godwiki/). We want to consider our approach with respect to the behaviours of cloud computing, particularly the elasticity and the pay-as-you-go model. Indeed, while rewriting queries may help to maximize the cache content avoiding evaluations to occur on the servers and thus to save money it may lead to longer response time especially when myriad of cloud instances are used. We would like to consider our approach with other types of dependencies, for example, conditional dependencies.

Acknowledgments. This work is partially supported by the STIC Asia project GOD (http://home.isima.fr/god/godwiki/). We would like to sincerely thank all the colleagues at ETIS, LIMOS and LRI laboratories for the interesting discussions.

References

1. Amazon. Dynamodb. Web page. http://aws.amazon.com/dynamodb/
2. Amazon. Rds. Web page. http://aws.amazon.com/rds/
3. Amazon. Simpledb. Web page. http://aws.amazon.com/simpledb/
4. Apache. Hadoop. Web page. http://hadoop.apache.org/
5. Armbrust, M., Fox, A., Griffith, R., Joseph, A.D., Katz, R.H., Konwinski, A., Lee, G., Patterson, D.A., Rabkin, A., Stoica, I., Zaharia, M.: A view of cloud computing. Commun. ACM **53**(4), 50–58 (2010)
6. Beyer, K.S., Ercegovac, V., Gemulla, R., Balmin, A., Eltabakh, M.Y., Kanne, C. - C., Özcan, F., Shekita, E.J.: Jaql: a scripting language for large scale semistructured data analysis. PVLDB **4**(12), 1272–1283 (2011)
7. Chaiken, R., Jenkins, B., Larson, P.Å., Ramsey, B., Shakib, D., Weaver, S., Zhou, J.: Scope: easy and efficient parallel processing of massive data sets. PVLDB **1**(2), 1265–1276 (2008)
8. Chen, L., Rundensteiner, E.A., Wang. S.: XCache: a semantic caching system for XML queries. In: SIGMOD, Madison, Wisconsin, USA, p. 618 (2002)
9. Chidlovskii, B., Borghoff, U.M.: Semantic caching of web queries. VLDBJ **9**(1), 2–17 (2000)

10. Dar, S., Franklin, M.J., Jonsson, B.T., Srivastava, D., Tan, M.: Semantic data caching and replacement. In: VLDB, Bombay, India, pp. 330–341 (1996)
11. Dash, D., Kantere, V., Ailamaki, A.: An economic model for self-tuned cloud caching. In: ICDE, Shanghai, China, pp. 1687–1693 (2009)
12. Dean, J., Ghemawat, S.: MapReduce: simplified data processing on large clusters. In: OSDI, San Francisco, California, USA, pp. 137–150 (2004)
13. d'Orazio, L., Traore, M.K.: Semantic cache for pervasive grids. In: IDEAS, Cetraro, Italy, pp. 227–233 (2009)
14. Halevy, A.Y.: Answering queries using views: a survey. VLDBJ **10**(4), 270–294 (2001)
15. Kantere, V., Dash, D., Gratsias, G., Ailamaki, A.: Predicting cost amortization for query services. In: SIGMOD, Athens, Greece, pp. 325–336 (2011)
16. Keller, A.M., Basu, J.: A predicate-based caching scheme for client-server database architectures. VLDBJ **5**(1), 35–47 (1996)
17. Laurent, D., Spyratos, N.: Rewriting aggregate queries using functional dependencies. In: MEDES, San Francisco, CA, USA, pp. 40–47 (2011)
18. Lillis, K., Pitoura, E.: Cooperative xpath caching. In: SIGMOD, Vancouver, BC, Canada, pp. 327–338 (2008)
19. Microsoft. Sql azure. Web page. http://www.windowsazure.com/en-us/home/features/data-management/
20. Olston, C., Reed, B., Srivastava, U., Kumar, R., Tomkins, A.: Pig latin: a not-so-foreign language for data processing. In: SIGMOD, Vancouver, BC, Canada, pp. 1099–1110 (2008)
21. O'Neil, P., O'Neil, E., Chen, X., Revilak, S.: The star schema benchmark and augmented fact table indexing. In: Nambiar, R., Poess, M. (eds.) TPCTC 2009. LNCS, vol. 5895, pp. 237–252. Springer, Heidelberg (2009)
22. Silva, Y.N., Larson, P.-A., Zhou, J.: Exploiting common subexpressions for cloud query processing. In: ICDE, Washington, DC, USA, pp. 1337–1348 (2012)
23. Thusoo, A., Sarma, J.S., Jain, N., Shao, Z., Chakka, P., 0002, N.Z., Anthony, S., Liu, H., Murthy, R.: Hive - a petabyte scale data warehouse using hadoop. In: ICDE, Long Beach, California, USA, pp. 996–1005 (2010)
24. Upadhyaya, P., Balazinska, M., Suciu, D.: How to price shared optimizations in the cloud. PVLDB **5**(6), 562–573 (2012)
25. Vancea, A., Machado, G.S., d'Orazio, L., Stiller, B.: Cooperative database caching within cloud environments. In: Sadre, R., Novotný, J., Čeleda, P., Waldburger, M., Stiller, B. (eds.) AIMS 2012. LNCS, vol. 7279, pp. 14–25. Springer, Heidelberg (2012)

Information Discovery

Do Stock Analysts Make Good Recommendations: A Unified System for Analysts' Performance Tracking and Ranking

Chaiyakorn Yingsaeree, Anon Plangprasopchok[(⊠)], Paramet Tanwanont, and Rattapoom Tuchinda

National Electronics and Computer Technology Center,
112 Thailand Science Park, Phahonyothin Rd.,
Klong Luang, Pathumthani 12120, Thailand
{chaiyakorn.yingsaree,anon.plangprasopchok,
paramet.tanwanont,rattapoom.tuchinda}@nectec.or.th

Abstract. Stock analyst's report is among of several important information sources for making investment decisions, as it contains relevant information about stocks as well as recommendation where investors should buy or sell the stock together with entry and exit strategies. Good analysts should often make trustworthy recommendations so that traders following them can make regularly profits from their advices. Nevertheless, identifying good analysts is not a trivial task especially when processed manually. Particularly, one has to collect and *extract* strategies from *unstructured texts* appearing in analyst reports, *backtest* such strategies with historical market data, and summarize backtested results by overall profits and losses. To address these problems, we propose a unified system which makes use of a combination of information integration and computational finance techniques to automate all these tasks. Our system performs considerably well in extracting recommendations from various analysts' reports and provides new valuable information to traders. The system has been made available online as a mobile application for community use.

Keywords: Information extraction · Information integration · Financial market data · Computational finance

1 Introduction

A stock analyst's report is used by many traders for making investment decisions; it contains relevant information about the stock in question as well as a recommendation whether investors should buy or sell the stock. In Thailand, two pieces of consumer research [1,8] into the stock trading behavior concludes that most investors relies on fundamentals and analyst reports, when trading.

Each day, several financial institutions release about 100 reports to help investors keep track of latest business development. Unfortunately, these reports

A. Kawtrakul et al. (Eds.): ISIP 2013, CCIS 421, pp. 45–56, 2014.
DOI: 10.1007/978-3-319-08732-0_4, © Springer International Publishing Switzerland 2014

are scattered among several websites, which make it difficult for investors to monitor new development. In addition, these reports often provide different estimates and recommendations. To find out which report has the most useful information, investors need to excruciatingly analyze them manually. To address these issues, we aimed to develop a system that (a) utilizes computer sciences techniques to track stock analyst reports from the Internet and (b) integrate financial knowledge into the system to evaluates their past performance.

In this paper, we describe StockGuru, a system that automatically tracks stock analysts' reports and evaluates their past performances. Our contribution is beneficial to the community in two folds. First, we demonstrate how to apply information integration and computational finance techniques to solve real-world problems. Second, StockGuru, which is publicly available in the iTunes Appstore, acts as another valuable source of information that helps traders decide which analysts to trust and track new reports to make trading decisions in a timely manner. Interestingly, the analyst performance evaluation result indicates that, on average, traders cannot generate excess return by blindly trading according to what stock analysts said. However, it also suggests that traders may be able to generate some profit if they choose to follow a decent one.

The rest of the paper is organized as follows. Section 2 reviews related work in the field of information integration and computational finance. Section 3 provides an overview of our analyst rating system. Section 4 shows how we extract data from unstructured data sources. Section 5 details the methodology to evaluate the performance of each analyst. Section 6 summarizes the result using real world data set from the Thailand Stock Exchange. Finally Sect. 7 highlights our contributions and lists possible future research directions.

2   Related Work

Previous works studying the performance of stock analysts provided both positive and negative results. For example, Stickel [9] analyzed the performance of stock analysts in New York Stock Exchange (NYSE) and American Stock Exchange (AMEX) and found that when stock analysts upgraded their recommendation to "Buy", the upgraded stocks increased 1.16 % in eleven days on average, while the stocks downgraded by analysts to Sell decrease −1.28 % in eleven days. Additionally, change of recommendation from bigger firms trends to have more effect than that of smaller ones.

Womack [10] analyzed 1,573 change of recommendation records of 882 companies between 1989 and 1991, and found that an average return of the companies that received an upgrade was 2.4 % while an average return of the companies that received a downgraded was −9.1 %. Womack described that this return asymmetry might be caused from the fact that analysts issued more upgrades than downgrades and they downgraded their recommendations only when necessary as negative recommendations generally impact their relationship with the downgraded companies.

Similarly, Desai and Jain [4] analyzed stock recommendations from top analysts who were invited to join Barron's Annual Roundtable between 1968 to 1991.

Their results indicated that the return generated from buying stock according to their recommendations was not significantly different from zero. Specifically, the average return for holding recommended buy stocks for 25 days to 75 days after the recommendation was released to the public were reduced from 0.33 % to −0.71 %. However, the results for sell recommendations was intriguing as the price of recommended sell stocks reduce −8.12 % on average. Consequently, they concluded that buy recommendations from these analysts did not have any investment value, while sell recommendations have some investment value.

The example of the work providing positive result for buy recommendations was Barber et al. [2] who investigated whether investors can made profit from stock analysts' recommendations. To achieve this, they constructed five virtual portfolios according to analysts' recommendations (i.e. strong buy, buy, hold, sell, and strong sell) and rearranged these portfolio daily to make it conform to current analysts' recommendations. The result indicated that the strong buy portfolio has 4.2 % excess return, while the strong sell portfolio has −7.6 % excess return. This suggested that investors can made 11.8 % excess return by buying strong buy portfolio and selling strong sell portfolio. However, when accounting for transaction cost this excess return reduced to only 2.5 %.

There are a number of prior works in information extraction to automatically extract information from texts. Basically, these works proposed techniques to construct a "wrapper" – a set of rules that scrape specific pieces of relevant information from document content. Depending on a structure of documents, the rules can be constructed from document "landmarks" such as delimiters and HTML tags [6] or linguistic patterns [3]. In the financial domain, Lee and Geierhos [5], for example, presented a linguistic-based information extraction approach that extract analysts' stock ratings information from analysts' report for statistical decision making. Their system recognized organization names (e.g. BASF, BMW, Ericsson), analyst houses (e.g. Gartner, Citigroup, Gold man Sachs), ratings (e.g. buy, sell, hold, underperform) and price estimation by using lexicalized finite-state graphs. Then, extracted company names and their acronyms have to be cross-checked against data the analysts provide. Finally, all extracted values are compared and presented into charts with different views depending on the evaluation criteria.

3   System Overview

To analyze and rank analysts' performances, our system has several modules to collect, extract and analyze stock information as shown in Fig. 1. Specifically, we developed a set of crawler modules to retrieve the following information: (1) company information, (2) company announcement, and (3) end-of-day stock price and (4) analysts' recommendations. Company information contains basic information of each individual company such as symbol name, company name, and the industry and business sector that the company operates in. Company announcement includes information about cash and share distributions, rights offering and shareholders meeting schedules. We use this information to adjust

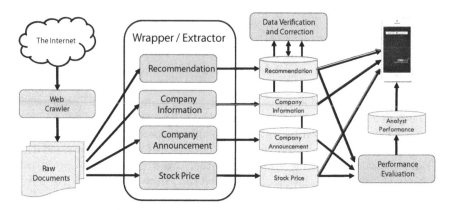

Fig. 1. This figure depicts the overview of a unified framework for analysts' performance tracking and ranking. The system firstly collects and extracts analyst recommendations, company information, company announcement and end-of-day stock price from the Web. It then evaluates and ranks each analyst based on the average profit one would gain from trading according to their recommendations.

historical stock price so that it reflects all the changes made to the company. The third information type, i.e. end-of-day stock prices, is used to calculate profit and loss obtained from trading according to what analysts recommended. In Thailand, this information has been curated and made publicly available on the Internet by the stock exchange of Thailand (SET) via http://www.set.or.th and http://www.settrade.com. The first three information types are available in well-structured forms as shown in Fig. 2. Particularly, they are tabular with a fixed number of columns, which can be programmatically scraped manually or using machine learning based techniques, e.g., [7]. Unfortunately, analysts' recommendations are generally in a free-text form which cannot easily be extracted automatically. We will describe their traits and our proposed solution to extract them automatically in more details in Sect. 4.

Since analysts' recommendations are produced by different analysts, the extracted data are occasionally erroneous due to human errors, such as typos, and extractor errors. The verification module that uses knowledge about relationships between stock prices can effectively identify such errors. Moreover, it can notify a system administrator when extracted data need correction or when the corresponding wrappers need an update. Subsequently, the system simulates trades according to entry and exit strategies from extracted recommendations. Analysts' performances are measured by the average profit gained from such simulated trades.

Once analysts' performances have been computed, the system will construct rankings for all analysts based on their performance on each specified stock, business sector and industry. These rankings are very useful for traders because a new recommendation from "good" analysts can be used as a new trading idea. As by-products of the ranking process, extracted recommendations are

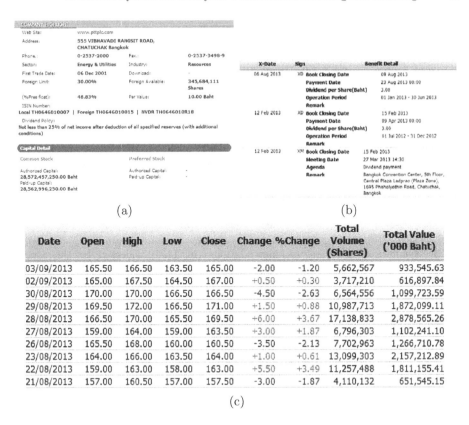

(a)

(b)

Date	Open	High	Low	Close	Change	%Change	Total Volume (Shares)	Total Value ('000 Baht)
03/09/2013	165.50	166.50	163.50	165.00	-2.00	-1.20	5,662,567	933,545.63
02/09/2013	165.00	167.50	164.50	167.00	+0.50	+0.30	3,717,210	616,897.84
30/08/2013	170.00	170.00	166.50	166.50	-4.50	-2.63	6,564,556	1,099,723.59
29/08/2013	169.50	172.00	166.50	171.00	+1.50	+0.88	10,987,713	1,872,099.11
28/08/2013	166.50	170.00	165.50	169.50	+6.00	+3.67	17,138,833	2,878,565.26
27/08/2013	159.00	164.00	159.00	163.50	+3.00	+1.87	6,796,303	1,102,241.10
26/08/2013	165.50	168.00	160.00	160.50	-3.50	-2.13	7,702,963	1,266,710.78
23/08/2013	164.00	166.00	163.50	164.00	+1.00	+0.61	13,099,303	2,157,212.89
22/08/2013	159.00	163.00	158.00	163.00	+5.50	+3.49	11,257,488	1,811,155.41
21/08/2013	157.00	160.50	157.00	157.50	-3.00	-1.87	4,110,132	651,545.15

(c)

Fig. 2. Illustrative examples on information available on SET (Stock Exchange of Thailand) website: (a) company information, (b) company announcement and (c) end-of-day stock price.

indexed according to stock symbols, endowing traders with an ability to quickly retrieve relevant recommendations, from various analysts, to a specific symbol they currently follow.

The following sections will describe two important modules: a wrapper for extracting unstructured analyst recommendations in Sect. 4 and an evaluator for computing analysts' performances in Sect. 5.

4 Unstructured Data Extraction

This section describes a method for extracting relevant information from analysts recommendation. Although the recommendations curated by the Stock Exchange of Thailand cover both technical and fundamental aspects of a particular stock, this paper will focus only on technical recommendations as they contain more information and are more challenging to extract than fundamental

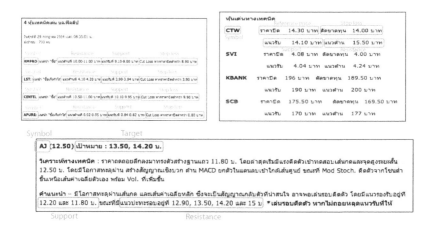

Fig. 3. Example of analysts' recommendations (in Thai) collected by the Stock Exchange of Thailand. Blue rounded rectangles with annotations indicate the relevant and actionable information that traders are interested in (Color figure online).

recommendations[1]. Consequently, the method proposed here for technical recommendations can be easily modified for fundamental recommendations.

4.1   The Nature of Stock Recommendations

Technical recommendations are generally in free-text forms as depicted in Fig. 3. One notable feature is that one article may contain several recommendations and there is no specified delimiters for separating one recommendation from the others. Additionally, the pattern that each analyst used to present their recommendations can be very different. For example, the recommendation in the top left corner of the figure mentions the resistance level before support and stop-loss prices while the one in the top right corner mentions stop-loss price before support and resistant levels. Furthermore, most of these recommendations are composed of phrases and numbers rather than proper sentences and there is no *HTML* tags or consistent delimiters that we can utilize to layout their boundaries. These characteristics make it difficult to generate wrappers based on linguistic patterns as in Lee and Geierhos [5] and machine learning techniques (e.g., STALKER [6] and Amilcare [3]). Such techniques require a considerable number of labeled data, especially when there are many possible patterns as in our case.

4.2   Heuristic-Based Wrappers

Instead of using machine learning approaches, we developed a wrapper that uses a simple heuristic rule along with a set of pattern matching rules and a

---

[1] Fundamental recommendations generally contain only rating information and earning estimates while technical recommendations also contain entry price, target price and stop-loss price as well as support and resistant levels.

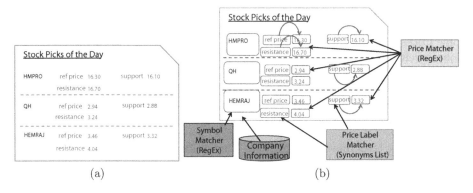

Fig. 4. This figure depicts (a) a hypothetical analyst recommendation article used for explaining key observations; (b) a schematic view of how the proposed heuristic-based wrapper works.

reference set. Our approach is based on 3 key observations as follows. Firstly, one can use stock symbol as a marker for separating one recommendation from the others. Consider a hypothetical recommendation article having 3 recommendations as illustrated in Fig. 4(a). We found that each individual recommendation starts with a stock symbol. If we scan the article and hit the symbol *QH*, we can infer that all information after the *QH* symbol should not belong to the recommendation of the previous symbol, *HMPRO*. Secondly, an individual symbol will be followed by other information such as support/resistant levels and stop-loss/target prices. Lastly, numerical value and their associated labels are always adjacent to each other. For example, the reference price of *HMPRO* is 16.30 because it is closest to the label "ref price".

From the observations above, we proposed a heuristic based wrapper as illustrated in Fig. 4(b). Basically, the wrapper firstly identifies symbols by using a regular expression to match candidate strings that might be symbol names. Then, each candidate string will be checked against the reference set, extracted from company information mentioned earlier in Sect. 3. The candidate existing in the set will be treated a symbol of the recommended company and is a starting point of a new recommendation. For each recommendation chunk, the wrapper further scans for all prices using a regular expression. Subsequently, the wrapper inspects all possible labels in the chunk by matching its individual sub strings to the price-label synonym list[2]. Matched labels are then assigned to the closest prices so that each recommendation has its prices annotated. Finally, each recommendation will be stored in a tuple (relational) form, comprising the following mandatory fields: "symbol", "quoted date", "reference price", "support", "resistance", "target price", into a database.

---

[2] The synonym list created by a system administrator is composed of price types and their alias names. For example, the reference price has "ref.price", "close price" as its aliases.

4.3   Data Verification

Some prices in a tuple of extracted recommendation may have their values anomalous or left blank. Such recommendation cannot be evaluated yet and required some attention from a system administrator. Consequently, we implemented the data verification process that exploits domain knowledge about stock prices and the market data at the time the recommendation was released. Intuitively, for a particular recommendation, its prices should meet all of the following criteria:

- the support level must be lower than the resistance level,
- the stop-loss price of a buy (sell) recommendation must be lower (greater) or equal to the support (resistant) level,
- the target price of a buy (sell) recommendation must be higher (lower) than support (resistant) level,
- the recommended entry prices should not be much different from the market prices.

Such simple yet effective rules help the system filtering out "non-actionable" recommendations and notify a system administrator for further investigations.

The wrapper and validation modules mutually perform considerably well in practice for all recommendation patterns from SET data. The performance of the system will be presented in more details in Sect. 6.

5   Analysts' Performance Evaluation

To determine whether analysts make profitable recommendations, we perform a trading simulation to see what will happened if we trade according to each recommendation. Specifically, for each recommendation extracted from the extractor, we perform the following simulation steps:

1. *Determine target and stop-loss prices.* If the recommendation does not contain specified target or stop-loss prices, we will infer these prices from support and resistant levels indicated in the recommendation. Particularly, for buy (sell) recommendations, we will utilize a resistant (support) level as a target price, while we will utilize a support (resistant) level as a stop-loss price. If the recommendation does not contain support and resistant level, we will treat this recommendation as non-actionable and do not perform a trading simulation on it.
2. *Enter into the position at a specified entry price.* If the recommendation does not contain an entry price, we will enter into the position at the next day opening price. However, when the recommendation specifics an entry price, we will wait to entry into the position when the price reaches the specified level. When the stock price hits target or stop-loss levels before we get into the position, we will treat the recommendation as non-actionable and do not perform trading simulation on it.

3. *Hold the position until stock price reach target or stop-loss prices.* After the stock price reaches target or stop-loss levels, we will exit the position at those prices. Specifically, if the stock price hits the target price before reaching the stop-loss price, we will exit the position at the target price and made a profit equal to the different between target and entry prices minus the transaction cost[3]. Similarly, if the stock price reaches the stop-loss price before hitting the target price, we will exit the position with a loss at the stop-loss price.

6   Empirical Validations

This section discusses the real-word data set for evaluating our framework, followed by the performance of the wrapper on extracting recommendations from unstructured analyst reports. We also reported analysts' performances in Thailand stock market during the past two and a half years, as well as briefly introduced *StockGuru* – an application platform realizing the proposed system.

6.1   Validation Data Set

The technical recommendations analyzed in this paper encompass the period from January 2011 to September 2013. This whole dataset contains 19, 274 recommendations from 20 analysts. Table 1 provides descriptive statistics of these recommendations. The information indicates that these analysts trend to issue buy recommendations more than sell recommendations. In fact, only 9 out of 20 analysts issue sell recommendations and the number of sell recommendations is only 6.3 % out of the whole dataset. Note that this is in lined with the evident from previous researches discussed in Sect. 2.

Table 1. Descriptive statistics of stock recommendations from 20 analysts between January 2011 to September 2013. The statistics indicates that analysts trend to issue buy recommendations more than sell recommendations.

Analyst	No. Buy	No. Sell	Total	Analyst	No. Buy	No. Sell	Total
A01	1617 (82.0 %)	354 (18.0 %)	1971	A11	954 (100 %)	-	954
A02	1271 (93.7 %)	85 (6.3 %)	1356	A12	900 (99.7 %)	3 (0.3 %)	903
A03	749 (59.1 %)	519 (40.9 %)	1268	A13	813 (97.2 %)	23 (2.8 %)	836
A04	1258 (100 %)	-	1258	A14	811 (100 %)	-	811
A05	1251 (100 %)	-	1251	A15	810 (100 %)	-	810
A06	1120 (90.5 %)	118 (9.5 %)	1238	A16	797 (100 %)	-	797
A07	1082 (92.2 %)	92 (7.8 %)	1174	A17	663 (100 %)	-	663
A08	1086 (99.1 %)	10 (0.9 %)	1096	A18	378 (100 %)	-	378
A09	1076 (99.4 %)	7 (0.6 %)	1083	A19	311 (100 %)	-	311
A10	1070 (100 %)	-	1070	A20	46 (100 %)	-	46
				Total	18063 (93.7 %)	1211 (6.3 %)	19274

---

[3] This paper sets commission at 0.17 % of total transaction cost for all simulations.

Table 2. The performance of the proposed heuristic-based wrapper and the profits and losses gained from following analysts' recommendations.

Analyst	No. Records			Performance			Win		Loss		Non-actionable
	Total	W/o Err.	Err.	%Win	PNL.Avg (%)	PNL.Var (%)	No.	PNL.Avg (%)	No.	PNL.Avg	
A01	1971	1759	212	54.64	0.21	0.23	801	4.04	665	−4.39	293
A02	1356	1170	186	55.71	0.27	0.23	615	3.78	489	−4.15	66
A03	1268	729	539	34.29	−0.25	0.24	250	5.60	479	−3.30	-
A04	1258	1198	60	15.56	−0.37	0.04	185	3.15	1004	−1.02	9
A05	1251	1214	37	30.56	−0.23	0.04	371	2.14	843	−1.27	-
A06	1238	1199	39	45.64	−0.03	0.18	513	3.95	611	−3.37	75
A07	1174	1071	103	44.63	−0.29	0.13	470	2.93	583	−2.89	18
A08	1096	1044	52	42.76	−0.25	0.17	437	3.55	585	−3.08	22
A09	1083	1022	61	43.78	−0.35	0.15	440	3.25	565	−3.16	17
A10	1070	1055	15	36.87	−0.14	0.37	382	6.49	654	−4.01	19
A11	954	863	91	57.42	−0.29	0.22	495	3.14	367	−4.92	1
A12	903	378	525	43.94	−0.86	0.11	163	1.95	208	−3.06	7
A13	836	747	89	48.98	−0.15	0.08	360	2.21	375	−2.41	12
A14	811	798	13	44.62	−0.13	0.12	344	2.50	427	−2.24	27
A15	810	780	30	55.37	−0.19	0.11	428	2.03	345	−2.94	7
A16	797	779	18	42.38	−0.43	0.04	328	1.29	446	−1.70	5
A17	663	571	92	62.81	−0.09	0.13	358	2.21	212	−3.96	1
A18	378	374	4	44.29	−0.22	0.10	163	2.07	205	−2.05	6
A19	311	311	0	44.05	−1.41	0.22	137	2.88	174	−4.79	-
A20	46	46	0	56.52	3.17	0.97	26	10.57	20	−6.44	-
Total	19274	17108	2166	43.98	−0.18	0.16	7266	3.28	9257	−2.90	585

6.2   Unstructured Data Extraction

To measure the performance of the automatic data extraction engine, we utilized the framework proposed in this paper to extract recommendation information from 19, 273 recommendations. The results, as reported in Table 2, indicate that the proposed framework can extract 88 % of the recommendations (i.e. 17, 108 out of 19, 274 recommendations) without any errors. After analyzing the error, we found that 6 % of the problems are attributed to extracted recommendations containing invalid prices, 5 % are attributed to extracted recommendations containing invalid stock symbols, and 1 % are attributed to other errors such as invalid recommendation types and the extractor unable to extract mandatory information.

6.3   Analysts' Performances

After simulating all actionable recommendations, we aggregate the profit and loss (PNL) of the recommendations from each analyst and calculate the average PNL, the average PNL when the recommendation generates profit and the average PNL when the recommendation losses money. The results are illustrated in Table 2 indicating that, on average, trading according to analysts' recommendations cannot generate excess return as the average PNL per recommendation for all analysts is −0.18 % which is close to the loss from the transaction cost.

(a)   (b)   (c)

Fig. 5. Screenshots of StockGuru mobile application highlight the following features: (a) an overall analyst ranking, (b) multi-resolution rankings (based on segments and industries), (c) a notification system of new reports from followed analysts.

The result from each individual analyst indicates that analysts are not equal, as some of them (i.e. A01, A02 and A20) have positive PNL while others have negative PNL. This indicates that traders might have more edges if they follow these three analysts, while it is very likely for them to lose their hard earned money if they blindly follow recommendations from other analysts.

6.4 StockGuru

The proposed framework have been implemented and deployed on a public cloud so that analyst reports are actively aggregated, extracted and evaluated. We also developed a mobile application, publicly available in the iTunes Appstore. It can be reached through the link http://goo.gl/L4JAX1. A stock trader can use this application to track new recommendations from "good" analysts, who have been rated according to the framework we proposed.

Figure 5 highlights key features of the applications. In Fig. 5(a) the application ranks stock analysts from leading brokers in Thailand based on "averaged profit per trade" (PNL). The information about the number of recommendations led to profits and that led to deficits are also provided. In Fig. 5(b) the analyst performances can be filtered based on overall performance, a specific industry and segment as well as a certain symbol. In Fig. 5(c), the application allows users to follow specific analysts and it will notify users when a new report comes out or when the outcome of a recommendation (whether profiting or not) is realized.

7   Conclusions

We have developed a system, namely *StockGuru*, that aggregates, extracts and evaluates analysts' recommendations from unstructured data. The system performed considerably well in extracting analyst reports that have various patterns. From the validation data collected from Thailand stock market, 88 percent of all automatically extracted recommendations were actionable and used for evaluating how well analysts performed. Analysts were then ranked according to their performances for overall or specific to particular industries, business sectors or symbols that they made recommendations. The ranks indicated that some analysts performed significantly better than many others in certain sectors. We also developed and made a mobile application publicly available, allowing amatuer and veteran traders utilizing analysts' performances to help make trading decisions or generate new trading ideas.

For future directions, we would like to take market conditions into account, for improving the way we rank analysts. Specifically, it's interesting to see which analysts perform consistently well during periods with economic fluctuations. We would also like to study possibilities to develop a strategy that combines recommendations from several analysts, to generate more robust recommendations. Distilling recommendations and market-movement predictions from posts and comments on social media websites is another interesting research topic to pursue.

References

1. Banjongprasert, S., Isareeyapracha, K.: Investor research survey. Technical report, Capital Market Research Forum (2011)
2. Barber, B., Lehavy, R., McNichols, M., Trueman, B.: Can investors profit from the prophets? security analyst recommendations and stock returns. J. Finance **56**(2), 531–563 (2001)
3. Ciravegna, F.: Adaptive information extraction from text by rule induction and generalisation. In: Proceedings of the 17th International Joint Conference on Artificial intelligence, IJCAI'01, vol. 2, pp. 1251–1256. Morgan Kaufmann Publishers Inc., San Francisco (2001)
4. Desai, H., Jain, P.C.: An analysis of the recommendations of the superstar money managers at barron's annual roundtable. J. Finance **50**(4), 1257–1273 (1995)
5. Lee, Y.S., Geierhos, M.: Buy, sell, or hold? information extraction from stock analyst reports. In: Beigl, M., Christiansen, H., Roth-Berghofer, T.R., Kofod-Petersen, A., Coventry, K.R., Schmidtke, H.R. (eds.) CONTEXT 2011. LNCS, vol. 6967, pp. 173–184. Springer, Heidelberg (2011)
6. Muslea, I., Minton, S., Knoblock, C.: Stalker: learning extraction rules for semistructured. In: AAAI Workshop on AI and Information Integration (1998)
7. Pinto, D., McCallum, A., Wei, X., Bruce Croft, W.: Table extraction using conditional random fields. In: Proceedings of the 26th Annual International ACM SIGIR Conference on Research and Development in Information Retrieval, SIGIR '03, pp. 235–242. ACM, New York (2003)
8. Rungruengpon, W.: The strategy to changing the saving and investment behavior of people aged between 20 to 29 years old to invest more in stock exchange. Technical report, Thammasat Business School (2013)
9. Stickel, S.E.: The anatomy of the performance of buy and sell recommendations. Financ. Anal. J. **51**(5), 25–39 (1995)
10. Womack, K.L.: Do brokerage analysts' recommendations have investment value? J. Finance **51**(1), 137–167 (1996)

Towards Facilitating the Development of Monitoring Systems with Low-Cost Autonomous Mobile Robots

Einoshin Suzuki[1(✉)], Yutaka Deguchi[1], Daisuke Takayama[1], Shigeru Takano[1], Vasile-Marian Scuturici[2], and Jean-Marc Petit[2]

[1] Department of Informatics, ISEE, Kyushu University, Fukuoka, Japan
{suzuki,takano}@inf.kyushu-u.ac.jp,
{yutaka.kyushu,takayamaD}@gmail.com
[2] CNRS, INSA-Lyon, Université de Lyon, Lyon, France
{Marian.Scuturici,Jean-Marc.Petit}@insa-lyon.fr

Abstract. This paper presents our ongoing work towards facilitating the development of monitoring systems with low cost autonomous mobile robots by unifying techniques from data mining and databases. Such a system is less invasive to privacy, more flexible to changes, and more focused in its observation. However, it is subject to major obstacles which are diverse targets, massive data, and huge management cost. We explain the base techniques of a discovery robot coupled with service-oriented declarative system. We sketch our applications on fall risk discovery and point out some challenges to be addressed.

Keywords: Data mining robot · Continuous-service oriented DB · Autonomous mobile robot · Elderly monitoring

1 Introduction

Recent rapid advancement of consumer mobile robots, e.g., Eddie[1], TurtleBot2[2], has opened a new avenue for AI research and applications. We believe that a monitoring system based on low-cost autonomous mobile robots has a huge potential to our society. Compared to the prevailing monitoring systems based on fixed cameras, such a monitoring system is less invasive to privacy, more flexible to changes, and more focused in its observation. Its application is useful in various environments such as factories, stations, halls, museums, schools, offices, and homes. Especially we target elderly assistance at home [4,9] due to the high growth rates of older adults in many regions of the world [19].

There are three major obstacles in developing such a system: (1) diverse targets, (2) massive data, and (3) huge management cost. The targets of the monitoring vary significantly, e.g., each aged person has his/her own behaviors,

---

[1] http://www.parallax.com/product/28992
[2] http://www.turtlebot.com/

A. Kawtrakul et al. (Eds.): ISIP 2013, CCIS 421, pp. 57–70, 2014.
DOI: 10.1007/978-3-319-08732-0_5, © Springer International Publishing Switzerland 2014

habits, preferences, requirements, and prohibitions. The observed data by the robots are massive, e.g., under a typical setting, a Kinect device[3] [24] outputs an image file of about 4.5 MB in size every 1/30 s, which results in about 4.0 PB in 1 year. Management of multiple robots is still in its infancy, e.g., even preparing a demonstration of such a system in an exhibition requires considerable skill and labor. Therefore a monitoring system based on low-cost autonomous mobile robots lies in the frontier of AI research.

Existing works for facilitating the development of a system with autonomous robots can be classified into a declarative language based approach [5,18] and a machine learning based approach [1,21]. The former category typically relies on a domain specific language with an emphasis on either the service aspects [5] or the ontology aspects [18]. The latter category typically learns a mapping between a world state and actions by experience [21] and/or demonstration [1]. The former category lacks extensibility and the latter scalability, due to insufficient separation of the entities ("what") from the methodologies and the contexts ("how + why"), and limited adaptability to new situations, respectively. Obviously our target system requires at least an integration of both categories.

We have recently started a new bilateral project between Japan and France for facilitating the development of such a system. Our approach is unique as it unifies techniques from data mining and databases on autonomous mobile robots. We employ techniques of data stream mining [10], anomaly detection [2], and pattern extraction [12] to cope with the first two obstacles (diverse targets, massive data) mainly based on a discovery robot developed in Suzuki laboratory in ISEE, Kyushu University [27]. The third obstacle (huge management cost) will be resolved based on the service oriented declarative language SoCQ developed in the database group of the LIRIS laboratory [11,23]. Our anomaly detection for data stream observed by an autonomous robot effectively handles concept drifts and the service oriented declarative language exhibits high extensibility as a pervasive environment management system. The project brings new research topics to data mining such as pattern extraction for the decision making of an autonomous robot, anomaly detection under the management of a service oriented declarative language, and data stream mining in a closely interacting multiple-robot system. Unlike much larger EU projects which involve elderly assistance at home by robots [4,9], our project heavily employs state-of-the-art methods of data mining and databases, seeking for establishment of the interdisciplinary domain among the three fields. In this setting, many challenges need to be addressed, most of them being known for years: integration of data mining primitives into database management systems [3,20] or the interaction between SQL and statistical models [8].

The bilateral project has its root to a domestic project in Japan towards long-term monitoring by autonomous mobile robot. Our second application (fall risk discovery) shown in Sect. 5 can be regarded as a fruitful outcome of the positive interactions between the two projects.

---

[3] http://research.microsoft.com/en-us/projects/vrkinect/

May 2011@Fukuoka   Fall 2011@Fukuoka   April 2012@Fukuoka

Winter 2012@Fukuoka   Fall 2013@ Lyon   July 2013@Fukuoka

Fig. 1. Our mobile robots with the periods when the corresponding pictures were taken

The rest of this paper is organized as follows. Section 2 explains our autonomous mobile robots while Sect. 3 reviews our main base techniques employed in the projects. We describe our unified approach for the monitoring system with low-cost autonomous mobile robots in Sect. 4 and show its applications to fall risk discovery in Sect. 5. Section 6 concludes.

2   Autonomous Mobile Robots

The Japanese team has been working on machine learning and data mining for autonomous mobile robots for about five years [13–16,25,27,28]. Figure 1 shows various kinds of robots constructed or assembled by the Japanese team and one kind of robots assembled by the French team, with the periods when the corresponding pictures were taken.

In the Figure, there is a difference between the robots in the upper row and those in the lower row. The former robots have standard cameras as their eyes while the latter robots have Kinects as their eyes. Kinect is a wonderful device which enables the construction of a sophisticated robot vision system for monitoring persons at low cost. A Kinect for Windows costs about 25,000 Japanese Yen or 180 euro. It can take 30 frames per second and a frame in the applications presented in Sect. 5.2 mainly consists of a color image, a depth image, and a skeleton as shown in Fig. 2. A skeleton consists of 20 joints, each of which is represented by its status and its x, y, and z coordinates. Hence the posture of a person to be monitored is represented by a tree of 20 nodes, each of which is essentially a point in the 3D space.

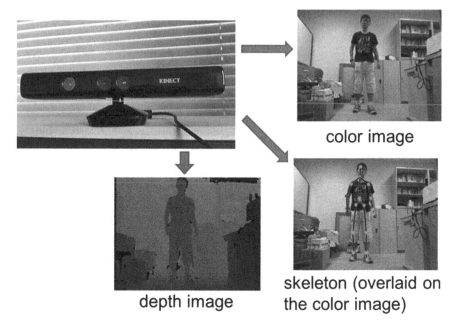

Fig. 2. Kinect for Windows and examples of data that it can measure (Color figure online).

3   Base Techniques

3.1   Discovery Robot

In the summer of 2011, the Japanese team built a discovery robot, which models the color distributions of the environment from millions of subimages and detects peculiar color distributions onboard, in real-time in an office [27]. The robot is able to fulfill the task of anomaly detection from data stream. It handles the data stream of subimages with a data index structure inspired by the clustering feature tree of BIRCH [30]. The data index structure is a core technique of data squashing, which is a method to allow the use of existing machine learning methods by scaling down the data [7].

Precisely speaking, an example in this abnormal detection based on online clustering corresponds to a subimage of $8 \times 8 = 64$ pixels and is represented by a bag of 31 kinds of colors. The 31 kinds of colors are a simplified version of color features [17] and consist of black, gray, white, and 28 kinds of achromatic colors, i.e., 4 kinds of (saturation, value) $\times$ 7 kinds of hue. The robot takes 1000 images in about 10 min, each image is of size 320×240 pixels and hence contains 1200 subimages each of size 8×8 pixels, resulting in 1.2 millions of examples observed and clustered in about 10 min. Figure 3 shows our discovery robot (left), an example of the detected anomaly (upper right), and the corresponding color

Fig. 3. Our discovery robot (left), an example of the detected anomaly (upper right), and the corresponding color image (lower right) (Color figure online).

```
1200000 <B:0.22, G:0.53, W:0.11, b4:0.05>
   1040522 <B:0.24, G:0.58, W:0.12>
      700603 <B:0.07, G:0.83>
      115196 <G:0.11, W:0.84>
      7430 <B:0.28, G:0.25, r4:0.20, p4:0.08>
      217293 <B:0.90, G:0.05>

   31092 <B:0.35, G:0.16, g4:0.05, b4:0.17, p4:0.09>
      6349 <B:0.09, G:0.32, y4:0.06, g4:0.18, b4:0.11>
      996 <B:0.05, G:0.16, g4:0.17, c4:0.45, b4:0.06>
      21718 <B:0.46, G:0.12, b4:0.20, p4:0.08>
      317 <B:0.24, G:0.09, r4:0.39, b4:0.06, p4:0.10>
      1712 <B:0.07, G:0.07, r4:0.05, b4:0.08, p3:0.07, p4:0.64>

   84121 <B:0.10, G:0.22, b2:0.08, b4:0.43>
      8438 <G:0.30, W:0.23, b2:0.16, b4:0.16>
      72490 <B:0.11, G:0.21, b2:0.08, b4:0.48>
      3193 <G:0.16, g4:0.10, c2:0.07, c4:0.39, b2:0.06, b4:0.12>

   44265 <G:0.19, r4:0.15, o4:0.16, y4:0.24>
      13420 <G:0.16, r4:0.10, o2:0.06, o3:0.09, o4:0.37, y4:0.09>
      14553 <G:0.27, o4:0.06, y4:0.54>
      5259 <B:0.05, G:0.24, W:0.15, r4:0.16, o4:0.08, y2:0.05, y4:0.09>
      3221 <G:0.27, y4:0.30, g4:0.30>
      7812 <B:0.05, r3:0.10, r4:0.54, o3:0.06, o4:0.08, p4:0.08>
```

Fig. 4. Data index structure constructed by the robot with a parameter value setting appropriate for display purpose [27]. Colors less than 5 % were omitted from display.

image (lower right). The detected anomaly corresponds to the green document box in the color image.

Figure 4 shows an example of the data structure constructed by the robot with parameter value setting appropriate for display purpose [27]. Here display purpose means that we set the value of a parameter large enough to produce a small tree, which is adequate for displaying the resulting tree to convey basic ideas of the method. In the Figure, a line represents the number of subimages followed by the mean vector in $< >^4$. B, G, W, r, o, y, g, c, b, and p represent black, gray, white, red, orange, yellow, green, cyan, blue, and purple, respectively. The digit after a color is the identifier of the kind of (saturation, value). The number after each bin is the ratio of the bin to the $8 \times 8 = 64$ pixels in the subimage. Colors less than 5 % were omitted from display. After an inspection phase of 1 min, the robot reports examples that are highly dissimilar to the nearest leaf of the data index structure as anomalies.

3.2 Data-Centric Applications in Pervasive Environments

Developing robots' applications is a tedious task since developers have to cope with heterogeneous data and diverse communication protocols. The success of such applications depends on many factors, one of them being performance of data accesses, easy management of heterogeneous data, and appearing/disappearing distributed services. To address these challenges, we designed and implemented a middleware called UbiWare [23] whose overall goal is to facilitate application development for pervasive environments. The surrounding space is seen as a database-like environment whereas the heterogeneous entities and devices as data services that produce data. Basically, whenever a new robot or device has to be integrated by application developers, the main thing he/she has to do is to write some drivers that implement the UbiWare middleware.

To query the distributed data services and access their data, Ubiware is integrated with a data stream management system: the Service-oriented Continuous Query (SoCQ) engine [11]. This integration facilitates the development of complex applications for pervasive environments using declarative service-oriented continuous queries. These SQL-like queries combine conventional and non-conventional data, namely slower-changing data, dynamic streams and functionalities provided by services. A thorough comparison with state of the art programming techniques (data stream management + ad-hoc programming) has been performed in [26]

In a similar way to databases, SoCQ implements the notion of *relational pervasive environment*, composed of several *eXtended Dynamic Relations*, or XD-Relations. The schema of an XD-Relation is composed of real and/or virtual attributes [11]. Virtual attributes represent parameters of various methods, streams, etc., and may receive values through query operators. The schema of an XD-Relation is further associated with binding patterns, representing method invocations or stream subscriptions.

SoCQ includes service discovery capabilities in the query engine. The service discovery operator builds XD-Relations that represent sets of available services providing required data. For example, an XD-Relation KINECT could be the result of such an operator, and be continuously updated when new KINECT services become available and when previously discovered services become unavailable.

---

[4] In the original proposal [30], it is the add-sum of the corresponding examples but we replaced it with the mean vector for ease of comprehension.

We argue that a pervasive environment management system such as SoCQ/
Ubiware allows to simplify the development of new applications significantly [26].
Application developers have to focus on what they have to do and not on how they
have to do it, since the latter is precisely the job of the query processing module of
the pervasive environment management system (PEMS) to decide the best way
to obtain an answer from a pool of continuous queries. Moreover, services such
as robots may appear or disappear dynamically without impacting the developer:
this is the PEMS responsibility to take appropriate actions with respect to available services and its actual perception of the environment through the collected
data.

4   Unified Approach for the Monitoring System with Low-Cost Autonomous Mobile Robots

4.1   Unifying Different Perspectives

In Fig. 1, the 5 robots in the rightmost picture in the lower row are Turtle-
Bot2 with Kobuki[5]. A simple program developed by the Japanese team allowed
the robot to follow a student walking along a corridor in a building for about
150 s. The program controls the robot so that it tracks the hip center joint of
the student observed with its Kinect according to several pre-specified parameters. This fact gives an evidence of the excellent performance of the TurtleBot2
with Kobuki as robot platform compared with the hand-made robots previously
constructed by the Japanese team.

After a demonstration of the movie, a typical question will be "What kind
of software is controlling this physical device?". The answers may be multiple,
according to the observer's background, yielding the uniqueness of tackling the
interdisciplinary research of the data mining, databases, and robotics domains
in the bilateral project.

Some data miners would answer "a data mining platform" as the result of
the following reasoning. "The device is equipped with a Kinect and thus is able
to observe data. It has also a latest notebook PC, which is powerful enough to
execute even the latest data mining algorithms. Hence the device can discover
patterns from the data it observes, which may be called active data mining as
the robot can decide the data it observes based on the patterns it discovers.
Undoubtedly the device is a data mining platform."

Some database researchers would answer "a continuous service-oriented DB"
as a consequence of the following reasoning. "The device is equipped with a
Kinect and thus is able to generate data. It has also a latest notebook PC, which
is powerful enough to execute even the latest database management systems.
Hence the device can process queries issued to the data it generates, which
include continuous queries as it is providing a service of following the student.
Undoubtedly the device is a continuous service-oriented DB". In the remainder
of this paper, we show how this combination of atypical researchers results in
atypical outcomes.

---

[5] http://kobuki.yujinrobot.com/home-en/about/reference-platforms/turtlebot-2/

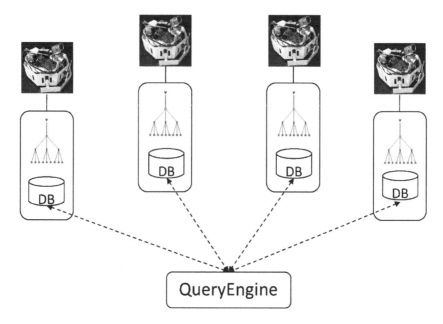

Fig. 5. Schematic diagram of the monitoring system with low-cost autonomous mobile robots.

4.2 Unified Approach

Figure 5 shows a schematic diagram of the monitoring system with low-cost autonomous mobile robots. The initial motivation of the monitoring system was to manage several data mining robots with a declarative stream data management system like SoCQ. The declarative query engine facilitates the interaction with multiple mobile robots. The robots are seen as components of a database, where each robot provides data (as streams) and functionalities (as services activating the actuators). Note that we adopted the essential part of the discovery robot and used it on our new robot platform equipped with a Kinect, i.e., TurtleBot2 with Kobuki.

Compared to the prevailing monitoring systems based on fixed cameras, such a monitoring system enforces a privacy policy. For instance, the robot can move away when the target wants to change his/her clothes using a gesture sign as a signal. The system is more flexible to changes, e.g., the robots just change their positions according to the layout of the furniture or change of habits of the target. Last but not least, the system is more focused in its observation because the robots can position themselves appropriately. Fixed cameras placed in the airports use pan, tilt, and zoom to focus on the suspicious targets, which is vulnerable to occlusions by obstacles. Mobile robots are less prone to such vulnerabilities.

Figure 6 shows the architecture of our unified approach, in which UbiWare [23], the middleware which facilitates application developments for ambient intel-

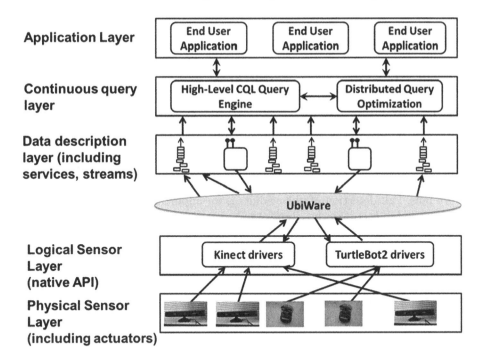

Fig. 6. Our multi-layered architecture.

ligence, connects the three top layers and the two bottom layers. The two bottom layers are the physical sensor layer and the logical sensor layer. The former includes the robots, sensors such as fixed Kinects, and actuators if any while the latter offers native APIs to the upper layers. The three top layers consist of the application layer, the continuous query layer, and the data description layer. The last one includes services and streams while the former two are self explanatory. The highest two layers are managed by SoCQ, which interacts with the robots and fixed cameras via *continuous queries* over the modeled environment.

The robots and the cameras build a local data index structure (a kind of the CF tree [30], as shown in Fig. 4). Locally processing the images and sharing the data index with SoCQ gives several advantages: 1. Handling massive observed data for better efficiency and energy consumption, 2. Denoising raw data with an adequate summarization, and 3. Offering a wide range of opportunities to optimize the query usage. Technically, SoCQ receives data observed by sensors as a data stream returned to a continuous query it issued. Each of the robots and other sensors and actuators, receives control commands from SoCQ as services. The communication is based on an HTTP-based protocol.

Each of the robots and fixed cameras manages the lowest two layers by updating extensions of the data index structure [27] according to the sensory inputs. The leaves of the data index structures can be considered as the squashed data [7], which are sent to the central controller as mentioned above. The squashed data also serve as the source data from which patterns are extracted.

The patterns are useful for effectively handling concept drifts and modeling the diverse targets/environment for an effective adaptation.

5   Fall Risk Discovery Applications

5.1   Elderly Falls

In the U.S., falls occur 30–60 % of older adults each year, and 10–20 % of these falls result in injury, hospitalization, and/or death [22]. Most falls are associated with identifiable risk factors, e.g., unsteady gait, and research shows that detection and amelioration of risk factors can significantly reduce the rate of future falls. Fall detection of older adults is an important problem of our aging society. The full report of the circumstances surrounding the fall is crucial in the post-fall treatment.

One of our long-term objectives is to provide a fall detection and reporting system using video cameras, audio sensors, and mobile robots. These devices are all connected (wired or wireless) to a central controller (a role played by a computer). The sensors are surveying a smart home, and for each detected fall a mobile robot is automatically sent in order to take a more detailed information about the event.

The monitoring process will be implemented as concurrent declarative continuous queries. For each task the query optimizer produces a physical execution plan based on existing services and context values.

5.2   Robot Applications

As a first step toward fall prevention of elderlies, a young student acted as the subject to avoid accidents. We modified the discovery robot to handle skeletons instead of color bags so that it detects anomalies which would possibly lead to falls [29]. The top row in Fig. 7 shows an example of the demonstration, though we use a different robot platform, i.e., TurtleBot2 with Kobuki, than in [29]. The key point of the application lies in its inter-skeleton distance, which captures the risk of falls. Experimental results in [29] are promising in terms of detection accuracy and subjective interpretations.

We have also implemented the unified approach in Sect. 4.2 with two robots and one desktop PC running SoCQ [6]. The two robots send their observed data to the desktop PC exploiting the functions of SoCQ and the desktop PC builds the index structure of the former application using the observed data. The development of the application was relatively fast thanks to the agile aspect of SoCQ. Unlike the first application, the robots, although still autonomous, follow the instructions issued by the desktop PC and the resulting clusters are maintained in the desktop PC, which corresponds to efficient distributed sensing. Experimental results in [6] are promising in terms of the positioning of the two robots. The bottom row in Fig. 7 shows an example of the demonstration.

The three major obstacles in developing a monitoring system based on low-cost autonomous mobile robots are circumvented or are going to be circumvented

First application (monitoring by a discovery robot)

Second application (fall risk discovery by 2 robots and a PC with SoCQ)

Fig. 7. Our two applications.

in these applications as follows. For the problem of diverse targets, both applications employ clustering as bases for adaptation. Obtained clusters depend on the targets and especially their behaviors, enabling the designer to better specify the appropriate reactions of the robot on the basis of agglomerated, similar sensory inputs. The problem of massive data has not been so far serious due to our hardware and software. Our robot platform, especially the Kinect device and the latest notebook PC, provides an effective means for measuring and storing massive data. The online clustering based on data squashing enables us to effectively handle more than millions of data under a reasonable setting, as clusters are updated with correct inter-cluster distances without the original data. Last but not least, for the problem of huge management cost, the initial development of a prototype system with a single robot and its extension to the current system with two robots were both felt relatively acceptable in terms of man-month in the Japanese team. Note that we do not argue that the cost was small, as several members of the Japanese team had to learn SoCQ developed by the French team and simultaneously construct a new system they never experienced. However, the fact that the system was developed in a few months mainly by the second author provides an evidence for justifying our proposal for facilitating the development of monitoring systems with low-cost autonomous mobile robots.

6   Conclusion

We have presented our ongoing Japanese-French project[6] for facilitating the development of monitoring system with low-cost autonomous mobile robots. The bilateral project has its root to a domestic project in Japan towards long-term monitoring by an autonomous mobile robot. Our approach integrates our anomaly detection/prevention from data stream and our service oriented declarative language on low-cost autonomous mobile robots, necessitating to cope with their

---

[6] http://liris.cnrs.fr/DSM4MR

limitations in a challenging but fruitful manner. The application of fall detection/prevention of older adults at home is significant in our ageing society, which is universal in these days. As a by-product, the project has a significance for serving as a first step toward unifying the research fields of data mining, databases, and robotics.

Our work tackles an interdisciplinary domain, as a cross fertilization of data mining and databases for autonomous mobile robots. The work is challenging because we are handling real-time, physical, and autonomous systems with latest techniques of the two domains. The Japanese team has also built a low-cost autonomous mobile robot which monitors a person in two offices [15,25], which would possibly serve as a basis for further development. We believe that research on realizing robots that monitor and discover is significant in the domains of AI and DB.

Acknowledgments. A part of this research was supported by a Bilateral Joint Research Project between Japan and France funded from JSPS and CNRS (CNRS/JSPS PRC 0672), and JSPS KAKENHI 24650070 and 25280085.

References

1. Argall, B., Chernova, S., Veloso, M.M., Browning, B.: A survey of robot learning from demonstration. Robot. Autom. Syst. **57**(5), 469–483 (2009)
2. Chandola, V., Banerjee, A., Kumar, V.: Anomaly detection: a survey. ACM Comput. Surv. **41**(3), 1–58 (2009)
3. Chaudhuri, S.: Data mining and database systems: where is the intersection? IEEE Data Eng. Bull. **21**(1), 4–8 (1998)
4. Coradeschi, S., et al.: GiraffPlus: combining social interaction and long term monitoring for promoting independent living. In: Proceedings of HSI 2013, pp. 578–585 (2013)
5. Datta, C., MacDonald, B.A., Jayawardena, C., Kuo, I.-H.: Programming behaviour of a personal service robot with application to healthcare. In: Ge, S.S., Khatib, O., Cabibihan, J.-J., Simmons, R., Williams, M.-A. (eds.) ICSR 2012. LNCS, vol. 7621, pp. 228–237. Springer, Heidelberg (2012)
6. Deguchi, Y., Takayama, D., Takano, S., Scuturici, V.-M., Petit, J.-M., Suzuki, E.: Integrating Service-oriented DBMS and Online Clustering on Multiple Autonomous Mobile Robots (under submission)
7. DuMouchel, W., Volinsky, C., Johnson, T., Cortes, C., Pregibon, D.: Squashing flat files flatter. In: Proceedings of KDD 1999, pp. 6–15 (1999)
8. Fang, L., LeFevre, K.: Splash: ad-hoc querying of data and statistical models. In: Proceedings of EDBT 2010, pp. 275–286 (2010)
9. Fischinger, D., Einramhof, P., Wohlkinger, W., Papoutsakis, K., Mayer, P., Panek, P., Koertner, T., Hofmann, S., Argyros, A., Vincze, M., Weiss, A., Gisinger, C.: HOBBIT - The mutual care robot. In: Proceedings of ASROB 2013 (2013) (in conjunction with IROS 2013)
10. Gama, J.: Knowledge Discovery from Data Streams. Chapman and Hall/CRC, Boca Raton (2010)
11. Gripay, Y., Laforest, F., Petit, J.-M.: A simple (yet powerful) algebra for pervasive environments. In: Proceedings of EDBT, pp. 359–370 (2010)

12. Han, J., Kamber, M., Pei, J.: Data Mining Concepts and Techniques. Morgan Kaufmann, San Francisco (2012)
13. Kouno, A., Montanier, J.-M., Takano, S., Bredeche, N., Schoenauer, M., Sebag, M., Suzuki, E.: Swarm robots that move in column formation based on rule discovery. In: Proceedings of 2011 IEEE/WIC/ACM International Conference on Intelligent Agent Technology (IAT 2011), pp. 556–557 (2011)
14. Kouno, A., Takano, S., Suzuki, E.: Constructing low-cost swarm robots that march in column formation. In: Dorigo, M., et al. (eds.) ANTS 2010. LNCS, vol. 6234, pp. 556–557. Springer, Heidelberg (2010)
15. Kouno, A., Takayama, D., Suzuki, E.: Predicting the state of a person by an office-use autonomous mobile robot. In: Proceedings of 2012 IEEE/WIC/ACM International Conference on Intelligent Agent Technology (IAT 2012), pp. 80–84 (2012)
16. Kumar, S., Nguyen Huy, T., Suzuki, E.: Understanding the behaviour of reactive robots in a patrol task by analysing their trajectories. In: Proceedings of 2010 IEEE/WIC/ACM International Conference on Intelligent Agent Technology (IAT 2010), pp. 56–63 (2010)
17. Lei, Z., Fuzong, L., Bo, Z.: A CBIR method based on color-spatial feature. In: Proceedings of TENCON 1999, pp. 166–169 (1999)
18. Lim, G.H., Suh, I.H., Suh, H.: Ontology-based unified robot knowledge for service robots in indoor environments. IEEE Trans. Syst. Man Cybern. Part A **41**(3), 492–509 (2011)
19. Lutz, W., Sanderson, W., Scherbov, S.: The coming acceleration of global population ageing. Nature **451**(7179), 716–719 (2008)
20. Ordonez, C., Pitchaimalai, S.K.: One-pass data mining algorithms in a DBMS with UDFs. In: Proceedings of SIGMOD 2011, pp. 1217–1220 (2011)
21. Peters, J., Vijayakumar, S., Schaal, S.: Reinforcement learning for humanoid robotics. In: IEEE-RAS International Conference on Humanoid Robots (2003)
22. Rubenstein, L.Z.: Falls in older people: epidemiology, risk factors and strategies for prevention. Age Ageing **35**, ii37–ii41 (2006)
23. Scuturici, V.-M., Surdu, S., Gripay, Y., Petit, J.-M.: UbiWare: Web-based dynamic data & service management platform for AmI. In: Middleware'12 13th International Middleware Conference (2012)
24. Shotton, J., Fitzgibbon, A., Cook, M., Sharp, T., Finocchio, M., Moore, R., Kipman, A., Blake, A.: Real-time human pose recognition in parts from single depth images. In: Proceedings of CVPR 2011, pp. 1297–1304 (2011)
25. Sugaya, S., Takayama, D., Kouno, A., Suzuki, E.: Intelligent data analysis by a home-use human monitoring robot. In: Hollmén, J., Klawonn, F., Tucker, A. (eds.) IDA 2012. LNCS, vol. 7619, pp. 381–391. Springer, Heidelberg (2012)
26. Surdu, S., Gripay, Y., Scuturici, V.-M., Petit, J.-M.: P-Bench: benchmarking in data-centric pervasive application development. In: Hameurlain, A., Küng, J., Wagner, R., Amann, B., Lamarre, P. (eds.) TLDKS XI. LNCS, vol. 8290, pp. 51–75. Springer, Heidelberg (2013)
27. Suzuki, E., Matsumoto, E., Kouno, A.: Data squashing for HSV subimages by an autonomous mobile robot. In: Ganascia, J.-G., Lenca, P., Petit, J.-M. (eds.) DS 2012. LNCS (LNAI), vol. 7569, pp. 95–109. Springer, Heidelberg (2012)
28. Takano, S., Loshchilov, I., Meunier, D., Sebag, M., Suzuki, E.: Fast adaptive object detection towards a smart environment by a mobile robot. In: Augusto, J.C., Collier, R., Keyson, D., Salah, A.A., Tan, A.-H., Wichert, R. (eds.) AmI 2013. LNCS, vol. 8309, pp. 182–197. Springer, Heidelberg (2013)

29. Takayama, D., Deguchi, Y., Takano, S., Scuturici, V.-M., Petit, J.-M., Suzuki, E.: Online Onboard Clustering of Skeleton Data for Fall Risk Discovery (under submission)
30. Zhang, T., Ramakrishnan, R., Livny, M.: BIRCH: a new data clustering algorithm and its applications. Data Min. Knowl. Disc. **1**(2), 141–182 (1997)

On Skill Acquisition Support
by Analogical Rule Abduction

Koichi Furukawa[1]([✉]), Keita Kinjo[2], Tomonobu Ozaki[3],
and Makoto Haraguchi[4]

[1] Graduate School of Business Innovation, Kaetsu University, Tokyo, Japan
`kfurukawa@kaetsu.ac.jp`
[2] College of Economics and Environmental Policy,
Okinawa International University, Ginowan, Japan
`keita.kinjo@okiu.ac.jp`
[3] College of Humanities and Sciences, Nihon University, Tokyo, Japan
`tozaki@chs.nihon-u.ac.jp`
[4] Graduate School of Information Science and Technology,
Hokkaido University, Sapporo, Japan
`makoto@kb.ist.hokudai.ac.jp`

Abstract. This paper describes our development of analogical abduction as an extension to our work on meta level abductive reasoning for rule abduction and predicate invention. Previously, we gave a set of axioms to state the object level causalities in terms of first-order-logic (FOL) clauses, which represent direct and indirect causalities with transitive rules. Here we extend our formalism of the meta level abductive reasoning, by adding rules to conduct analogical inference. We have applied our analogical abduction method to the problem of explaining the difficult cello playing techniques of spiccato and rapid cross strings of the bow movement. Our method has constructed persuasive analogical explanations about how to play them. We have used a model of forced vibration mechanics as the base world for spiccato, and the specification of the skeletal structure of the hand as the basis for the cross string bowing technique. We also applied analogical abduction to show the effectiveness of a metaphorical expression of "eating pancake on the sly" to achieve forte-piano dynamics, and successfully created an analogical explanation of how it works.

Keywords: Rule abduction · Analogical abduction · Predicate invention · Predicate identification · Cello playing

1 Introduction

Abduction is a kind of synthetic reasoning to construct explanatory hypotheses about surprising observations. Here we explain how we have succeeded in applying abductive inference to provide explanations about how to perform difficult

A. Kawtrakul et al. (Eds.): ISIP 2013, CCIS 421, pp. 71–83, 2014.
DOI: 10.1007/978-3-319-08732-0_6, © Springer International Publishing Switzerland 2014

cello playing techniques, by exposing previously "hidden secrets" behind what are sometimes called a "knack" for a particular technique.

Knacks play crucial roles in acquiring artistic or sports skills. Knacks are target-dependent and are expressed by such phrases as "if you want to achieve a target exercise A, you should do an action B". But typically it is difficult to explain why the action B works for achieving the exercise A because of the "hidden secrets" behind the knack.

This problem setting fits the abduction framework quite well. A knack is usually a surprising observation and therefore hypotheses generation by abduction can help in finding candidates for the "secret" prerequisite for achieving the given exercise. To elaborate, we try to abduce missing hypotheses to achieve the goal (exercise) A under the assertion of the fact (action) B. Since B appears at the leaf of the proof tree, the abduction procedure has to find hypotheses in between the goal A and the leaf B, identified as a (set of) rule(s). We refer to this abductive procedure as *rule abduction*. Rule abduction cannot be achieved by standard Abductive Logic Programming (ALP), because abducibles are limited only to facts in ALP. To solve the difficulty, we developed a rule abduction method using *m*eta level abduction [1,2].

However, our rule abduction alone is insufficient to obtain meaningful missing prerequisites in the real application domain of skill acquisition. For example, consider an example of a knack "you should bend the thumb joint to realize crossing strings quickly." In this example, a missing rule is the knack itself; that is, "to achieve crossing strings quickly, bend the thumb joint" is a rule to be hypothesized by rule abduction. But it is easy to see that this rule is useless, because it does not explain *why* it works effectively.

Here we introduce an analogical abduction system which makes it possible to give a suitable explanation to the proposed knack. To show the effectiveness of the knack, we need to identify a hidden reason. The hidden reason is typically provided by analogical reasoning which gives a possible explanation of the knack by means of an argument in an underlying analogical domain associated with the original vocabulary of the abducible rules. There may be a situation where a (set of) intermediate proposition(s) is necessary to fill a gap between the premise B of the knack and its goal A, in which case we need to invent a new node (predicate) between them.

Note that some studies, [3,4], discuss the relationship between analogy and abduction (or induction) to complete missing clauses. Defourneaux and Peltier [3] proposed to use abduction to hypothetically assume some clauses with which proofs in a base domain can be transformed into those in a target one. A major part of target domain for deduction is thus obtained by analogy, while some auxiliary clauses are supplemented by abduction to complete a proof in the target domain. In contrast with such a usage of abduction, abduction in this paper is to build similarity (correspondence) between graph vertices according to which causality (represented by graph edges) is transformed and guessed in the target domain.

A similar construction of target clauses can be also realized by inductive inference using positive and negative examples. A learning system presented in [4] calculates a major part of target program by applying hypothetical analogy mapping to a given set of program clauses of a base domain. After the mapping, a refinement operator of inductive inference is applied to the major part in order to have the target clauses so that the reasoned program clauses in the target domain are consistent with the examples. Neither induction nor abduction are not directly used to hypothetically assume analogy correspondence, similar to the case of [3].

There is another research which combines abduction and case-based reasoning [5]. They have tried to incorporate case-based reasoning into abductive logic programming and have succeeded in automatically finding pairs of similar objects by abduction. On the other hand, we focus analogous systems having causality where we try to identify corresponding objects having similar roles in their causality relations.

We consider three analogical abduction problems and propose possible procedures to give solutions. In Sect. 2, we give a summary of our previous work on rule abduction and predicate invention. In Sect. 3, we incorporate analogical inference into rule abduction. In Sect. 4, we show programs for the three concrete examples and their solutions. Finally in Sect. 5, we discuss several issues of our approach and give concluding remarks.

2 Rule Abduction and Predicate Invention

In this section, we give the summary of our previous research to realize rule abduction and predicate invention [1,2].

Definition 1. *Let B be a set of clauses representing background knowledge, and G a set of literals representing observed events. Consider a set Γ of literals that can be assumed to be true. Each member of Γ and any instance of an element of Γ is called an abducible literal, and the predicate of an abducible literal is called an abducible predicate.*

Given B, G, and Γ, abductive reasoning infers a set H of abducible literals such that

$$B \cup H \models G \tag{1}$$

$$B \cup H \text{ is consistent, and} \tag{2}$$

$$H \text{ is a set of instances of literals from } \Gamma \tag{3}$$

Then, H is called an explanation of G (with respect to B and Γ).

Each literal in H can contain variables, which are assumed to be existentially quantified. If H does not contain any variables, it is called a ground explanation.

In Definition 1, the first condition states that the observed event G can be explained by augmenting B with an additional hypothesis H. Because we use clausal theories instead of logic programs, an integrity constraint is represented

Fig. 1. An empirical causality representing that bending the thumb causes quick strings crossing

as a negative clause in B, and the second condition in Definition 1 corresponds to the satisfaction of integrity constraints.

SOL (Skip Ordered Linear) resolution [6] is a calculus that realizes abductive reasoning in full clausal theories, and SOLAR [7] is a tableaux-based implementation of SOL resolution.

To implement abductive reasoning with SOL resolution, we have to convert the first condition in Definition 1 into the following formula. This is an application of the relation known as inverse entailment.

$$B \cup \neg G \models \neg H \tag{4}$$

Since, both G and H can be regarded as conjunctions of literals, both $\neg G$ and $\neg H$ are clauses. On the other hand, the second condition in Definition 1 is equivalent to $B \not\models \neg H$. Hence, to compute an explanation of G in abductive reasoning, a theorem of B and $\neg G$ which is not a theorem of B is deduced as $\neg H$, which is then negated as H. In this case, since any element of H is an abducible literal, any literal in $\neg H$ is the negation of an instance of an element of Γ. Moreover, since any theorem $\neg H$ deduced from a clausal theory in SOL resolution is computed as a clause, every variable contained in it is universally quantified, and is thus existentially quantified in its negation H.

Suppose that we empirically know a cause s brings a remarkable result g. Here, s and g are called a *cause event* and a *result event*, respectively. This relation is actually an empirical causality whose example is given by Fig. 1. Our task of rule abduction is to explain why or how this causality holds, by finding an explanation that fills the gap between a causal event and a causal result.

A *causal graph* is a directed graph representing causal relations, and consists of a set of nodes and arcs. A *direct causal relation* corresponds to an arc, and a *causal chain* is represented by the reachability between two nodes.

When there is a direct causal relation from the node s to the node g, we declare that $connected(g, s)$ is true, shown by an atom (5). If we know that there is no direct causal link from s to g, we add an *integrity constraint* of the form (6).

$$connected(g, s) \tag{5}$$

$$\neg connected(g, s) \quad \bullet \tag{6}$$

When there is a *causal chain* from s to g, we declare that $caused(g, s)$ is true. We then have the following formulas as axioms:

$$caused(X, Y) \leftarrow connected(X, Y) \tag{7}$$

$$caused(X, Y) \leftarrow connected(X, Z) \wedge caused(Z, Y) \tag{8}$$

$caused(g, s).$ $\leftarrow connected(g, s)$

Fig. 2. An observed indirect causal relation and its clausal form representation (left), and a causal graph corresponding to a hypothesis with a new predicate (right).

Here, the predicates *connected* and *caused* are both meta-predicates for object-level propositions g and s. From now on, we refer to this representation of causality relations as Meta Level Causality (MLC) representation.

Rules, like causal relations at the object level, are represented by atoms in the meta level. In this way, we can implement *rule abduction* in the object level as *fact abduction* in the meta level.

When a causal graph has defect, there is no path between a goal event g and an input event s. Now an abductive task can be used to infer missing links (and sometimes missing nodes) to complete a path between the two nodes. This is done by setting the abducibles Γ as atoms containing connected only: $\Gamma = \{connected(\_,\_)\}$. The observation is given in the form of the causal chain $caused(s, g)$, but we usually assume that there is no direct causal relation between them, i.e., $\neg connected(g, s)$, otherwise we would not have needed abduction.

Suppose an observation $caused(g, s)$ is given together with a constraint $\neg connected(g, s)$. The clausal form of the observation and the constraint, and their corresponding causal graph are given in Fig. 2(left):

Within this specification, a possible explanation has the following form:

$$\exists X \, (\, connected(g, X) \wedge connected(X, s) \,) \tag{9}$$

This X can be unified with some known node in the causal graph, but if it is assumed as a new node, this assumption is equivalent to predicate invention [8]. See Fig. 2(right). Note here that, to introduce these kinds of explanations, we need to allow *existentially quantified formulas* as hypotheses. Abduction by SOLAR enables us to infer hypotheses having this form as stated above.

3   Analogical Abduction

In this section, we incorporate analogical reasoning into our MLC framework. We refer to the world under consideration as the target world and the corresponding analogical world as the base world. Analogical reasoning is achieved by introducing a base world similar to the target world, where we conduct inference [9]. Analogical reasoning can be formulated as logical inference with equality hypotheses [10]. We achieve analogical abduction by extending our MLC based rule abduction framework.

We modify the causality relationship formula (7) and (8) to deal with causalities in the different worlds separately as follows:

$$t\_caused(X, Y) \leftarrow t\_connected(X, Y) \tag{10}$$

$$t\_caused(X, Y) \leftarrow t\_connected(X, Z) \wedge t\_caused(Z, Y) \tag{11}$$

$$b\_caused(X, Y) \leftarrow b\_connected(X, Y) \tag{12}$$

$$b\_caused(X, Y) \leftarrow b\_connected(X, Z) \wedge b\_caused(Z, Y) \tag{13}$$

where the prefix "$t\_$" represents a predicate in the target world and "$b\_$" in the base world. Although the predicate "b_caused" does not appear in following examples, we define it because of the symmetry with "t_caused," for the possible future use.

We also introduce a predicate "$similar(X, Y)$" to represent similarity relations between an atom X in the target world and a corresponding atom Y in the base world.

Now we have to define the predicate "$t\_connected$," for which we have to consider three cases to show the connectedness in the target world; the first case is that the connectedness holds from the beginning, (14); the second case is that it holds by abduction as a solution of abductive inference, (15); and the third case is that it is derived by analogy, (16). Definition (16) contains an auxiliary predicate "$print\_connected\_by\_analogy(X, Y)$" which indicates that it is to be "$printed$" as a part of an abduced hypothesis to provide evidence that the analogical connection is actually used to show the "$t\_connected$"ness. Since analogical reasoning can be achieved without any defects in the inference path, we need to prepare an artificial defect, "$print\_connected\_by\_analogy(X, Y)$", on the path. This printing in turn is defined by specifying the predicate "$print\_connected\_by\_analogy$" as an abducible.

$$t\_connected(X, Y) \leftarrow connected\_originally(X, Y) \tag{14}$$

$$t\_connected(X, Y) \leftarrow connected\_by\_abduction(X, Y) \tag{15}$$

$$t\_connected(X, Y) \leftarrow connected\_by\_analogy(X, Y) \wedge$$
$$print\_connected\_by\_analogy(X, Y) \tag{16}$$

We have to further define three predicates; "$connected\_originally$", "$connected\_by\_abduction$" and "$connected\_by\_analogy$". The predicate "$connected\_originally$" is used in the assertion of facts representing the original connection; "$connected\_by\_abduction$" is introduced as an abducible predicate. Finally, the definition of "$connected\_by\_analogy$" is given by the following analogy axiom which plays a central role in analogical abduction.

Analogy Axiom

$$connected\_by\_analogy(X, Y) \leftarrow b\_connected(XX, YY) \wedge$$
$$similar(X, XX) \wedge similar(Y, YY) \tag{17}$$

This axiom states that the nodes X and Y in the target world can be linked by the predicate "$connected\_by\_analogy(X, Y)$" because of the base relationship

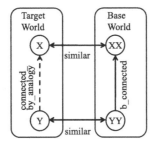

Fig. 3. A scheme representing the analogical axiom.

"*b_connected*(XX, YY)" between XX and YY which are similar to X and Y, respectively, as shown in Fig. 3. Note that there may be more than one similarity candidates. In this paper, we assume that the user provides some of the initial similarities, and that the abductive inference engine will compute any remaining possible similarity hypotheses to explain the observation.

Finally we state an important integrity constraint that *connected_by_abduction* and *connected_by_analogy* does not hold simultaneously as expressed as follows:

$$\leftarrow connected\_by\_analogy(X, Y) \wedge connected\_by\_abduction(X, Y) \qquad (18)$$

4   Analogical Abduction Examples

In this section, we show three analogical abduction examples in cello playing domain. The first one is a problem of discovering similarities to establish analogy between two given worlds. The second one is to conduct both predicate invention and similarity discovery at the same time. The third one is applying analogical abduction to metaphorical expression.

4.1   Discovering Similarities

We consider a problem of achieving the cello playing technique called spiccato, by analogy with forced vibration. Because of a cello instructor's suggestion, we happened to know that "holding the bow by the ring finger" is an essential action to achieve spiccato. In addition, from our intuition about the physics of such skills, we believe that the forced vibration is achieved by both "keeping the timing of energy supplying just after the maximum amplitude" and "absorbing shock of the energy supply." The similarity to be discovered here is the one between "holding the bow by the ring finger" and "absorbing shock of the energy supply." This similarity suggests that spiccato is achieved by holding the bow by the ring finger in order to absorb shock of hitting the bow to a string (to supply energy to the bow to bounce continuously). The relationship of the target world of achieving spiccato and the base world of forced vibration is shown in Fig. 4.

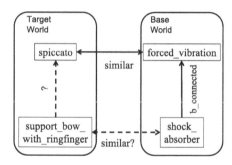

Fig. 4. Analogical abduction for achieving spiccato playing. The set of dotted lines are to be computed as a hypothesis.

The analogical abduction program is given as follow. We use Prolog-like notation here for the readability. In the program, the notation "Pred/N", such as connected_by_abduction/2, denotes a predicate "Pred" having "N" Arities.

% Observation (G) :

t_caused(spiccato, support_bow_with_ringfinger).   (19)

% Abducible predicates(Γ) :

abducibles([connected_by_abduction/2, similar/2,

print_connected_by_analogy/2]).

% Background Knowledge(B) :

%%% Base world:

b_connected(forced_vibration, shock_absorber).   (20)

%%% Target world:

:-connected_by_abduction(spiccato, support_bow_with_ringfinger).   (21)

% Similarity:

similar(spiccato, forced_vibration).   (22)

%Axioms:

b_caused(X, Y):-b_connected(X, Y).

b_caused(X, Y):-b_connected(X, Z), b_caused(Z, Y).

t_caused(X, Y):-t_connected(X, Y).

t_caused(X, Y):-t_connected(X, Z), t_caused(Z, Y).

t_connected(X, Y):-originally_connected(X, Y).

t_connected(X, Y):-connected_by_abduction(X, Y).

t_connected(X, Y):-connected_by_analogy(X, Y), print_connected_by_analogy(X, Y).

connected_by_analogy(X, Y):-b_connected(XX, YY), similar(X, XX), similar(Y, YY).

In this program, the goal (observation) to be satisfied is "t_caused(spiccato, support_bow_with_ringfinger)" (clause (19)). We provide the following two facts: (1) "shock_absorber" is one of the possible causes to achieve the forced vibration (clause (20)), and (2) spiccato is analogous to the forced vibration (clause(22)). In addition, we provide a negative clause asserting that the direct connection from "support_bow_with_ringfinger" to "spiccato" cannot be hypothesized (clause (21)).

In a SOLAR experiment, the number of obtained hypotheses is 7 when the maximum search depth is set to 10 and the maximum length of produced clauses is 4. One plausible hypothesis is:

$$\texttt{print\_connected\_by\_analogy(spiccato, support\_bow\_with\_ringfinger)} \land$$
$$\texttt{similar(support\_bow\_with\_ringfinger, shock\_absorber)}$$

which indicates that the support of the bow with the ring finger in achieving spiccato is analogous to the shock absorber in the forced vibration as shown in Fig. 4. Note that we gave a similarity between spiccato and forced_vibration and obtained another similarity between support_bow_with_ringfinger and shock_absorber by analogical abduction. It is note worthy to mention that we need not provide any definition of the "similar" predicate in abducing similarity predicates since they can be automatically obtained by the abduction engine which tries to fill gaps to make the proof of causality relation (19) complete.

4.2 Analogical Abduction with Predicate Invention

In this subsection, we consider the problem of showing the effectiveness of bending the thumb to realize the quick crossing of strings (cross_strings_quick). We use the skeletal structural linkage of the knuckle (of the first four fingers) and the thumb (b_connected(knuckle, thumb)) as a counterpart of a functional linkage of bending the knuckle and bending the thumb (t_connected(knuckle_bend, thumb_bend)) in the analogy setting. Note that we define the similarity only between "bending_thumb" and "thumb" without providing the predicate "ben _knuckle", which is to be invented by abductive reasoning. In this example, we conduct discovering missing similarities and invent a predicate at the same time. The problem structure is shown in Fig. 5.

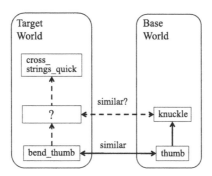

Fig. 5. Analogical abduction with predicate invention.

The abduction program for this problem is shown as follows (axiom clauses are omitted here as well):

% Observation(G) :

t_caused(cross_strings_quick, bend_thumb).

% Abducible predicates(Γ) :

abducibles([connected_by_abduction/2, similar/2,

print_connected_by_analogy/2]).

% Background Knowledge(B) :

%%% Base world:

b_connected(knuckle, thumb).

%%% Target world:

:-connected_by_abduction(cross_strings_quick, bend_thumb).

% Similarity:

similar(bend_thumb, thumb).

Under the same condition as before, we obtained 7 hypotheses, one of which is the following:

$$connected\_by\_abduction(cross\_strings\_quick, \_0) \wedge$$
$$similar(\_0, knuckle) \wedge$$
$$print\_connected\_by\_analogy(\_0, bend\_thumb)$$

This hypothesis accurately represents the structure shown in Fig. 5. We further conducted our experimental study by deleting the similarity relation "similar (bend_thumb, thumb)" from the above program and then succeeded in recovering this link as well.

4.3 Explaining the Effectiveness of Metaphorical Expression

To show the applicability of our approach to different kinds of problems other than mechanical models, we apply our analogical abduction to explain the effectiveness of a metaphorical expression. An example of metaphorical expression, issued by a trainer to achieve forte-piano dynamics in orchestra rehearsal, is "eating pancake on the sly," which means that one takes a big mouthful of pancake first, and then he/she tries to make it secret by a motion of imperceptible action of chewing. The difficulty of achieving such dynamics arises because we cannot control our muscle strength because of an inability to precisely estimate force. In addition, it is quite difficult to attain consensus amongst players about the shape of the dynamics envelope. But a metaphorical expression can sometimes help achieve a consensus. This phenomenon is formalized in terms of our analogical abduction framework.

Our goal is to prove "caused_by(forte_piano, eat_pancake_on_the_sly)". We assume that the expression "eating pancake on the sly" induces a sequence

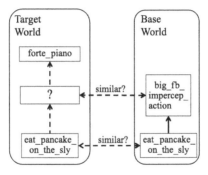

Fig. 6. Mataphorical expression of "eating pancake on the sly" to achieve forte-piano.

of motor control commands indicating a big action followed by an impercep-tible action ("big_fb_impercep_action") in the brain, which arises within the metaphorical base world (see Fig. 6). The analogical abductive reasoning is shown as follows:

% Observation(G) :

t_caused(forte_piano, eat_pancake_on_the_sly).

% Abducible predicates(Γ) :

abducibles([connected_by_abduction/2, similar/2,

$\qquad\qquad\qquad\qquad$ print_connected_by_analogy/2]).

% Background Knowledge(B) :

%%% Base world:

b_connected(big_fb_impercep_action, eat_pancake_on_the_sly).

%%% Target world:

:-connected_by_abduction(forte_piano, eat_pancake_on_the_sly).

Under the same condition as before, we obtained 6 hypotheses, one of which is the following:

$\qquad$ connected_by_abduction(forte_piano, _0) ∧

$\qquad\qquad$ similar(_0, big_fb_impercep_action) ∧

$\qquad$ similar(eat_pancake_on_the_sly, eat_pancake_on_the_sly) ∧

$\qquad\quad$ print_connected_by_analogy(_0, eat_pancake_on_the_sly)

Note that the entire problem structure of this analogical abduction is almost the same as our previous predicate invention example shown in Fig. 5 except for the treatment of the similarity relation on the bottom; it is abduced in the metaphorical analogy case whereas it is given from the beginning in Fig. 5. The characteristics of the metaphorical analogy is that the same analogical expression appears in both the base and the target worlds. Since a metaphorical expression directly induces emotional feeling to produce adequate motor control commands for achieving the given goal, it should be included in the target world; on the other hand, the same metaphorical expression triggers a similar motion in the eating action which means that it should be in the base world. Another remark is that the metaphorical expression of "eating pancake on the sly" plays the role of converting a quantitative direction of the sound volume adjustment into a qualitative one, which is much more intuitive and understandable to human.

5   Discussion and Future Work

In this paper, we proposed an approach of combining rule abduction and analogical reasoning by adding analogy axioms to the original causality relation axioms. We introduced the framework of defining the target world and the base world for the analogical setting as a part of the added analogy axioms.

We succeeded in demonstrating our new analogical abduction engine by applying it to three cello exercises to obtain analogical explanations: one is the similarity discovering problem between a predicate "holding the bow with ring finger" in the target world, and a predicate "absorbing shock" in the base world, as shown in Fig. 4; the second example uses both predicate invention and analogical reasoning to explain the invented predicate as shown Fig. 5, which is our original goal of this paper; and the final example shows the effectiveness of using metaphorical expression to achieve proper dynamics of forte-piano, as shown in Fig. 6. The last example shows the richness of our approach, which covers not only mechanical theories as the base world but also metaphorical expressions which inspire our brain.

Although we intended to incorporate analogical inference into abduction, we failed to achieve the introduction of "structural analogy," since our formulation considers substituting only single connectedness in the target world by the corresponding one in the base world. One possible realization of the structural analogy is to "import" parts of the proof tree in the base world inference into the target world. The essential problem is to introduce "and" connection of the proof tree in the base world into the target world's proof. For example, in our spiccato domain, the forced vibration is achieved by "keeping the timing of energy supplying just after the maximum amplitude" and "absorbing shock of the energy supply." Our attempt was to conduct analogical reasoning by focusing only the second condition of requiring a shock absorber. We will need a more elaborate formulation to deal with this problem.

There is another fundamental issue to be addressed to achieve more realistic analogical abduction. In this paper, we explicitly provide a base world analogous to the target world. In real problems for discovering or explaining skills, we may need to find an appropriate base world itself, before being able to conduct analogical reasoning, or to find and extract similar sub-worlds adequate for analogical abduction from the given target and base worlds. To deal with these problems, we have to provide detailed attributes to the components of each world and compute the degree of similarity for each pair of subset to find analogous pairs [11].

In this paper, we investigated possible ways to incorporate analogical reasoning with a well established ALP system SOLAR. In our approach, we put an abduction engine in the center and tried to add analogical reasoning on it. However, there are other possibilities to generalize our approach further to find better integration of abduction and analogy, including metaphor. One viewpoint is to make analogical reasoning propose adequate abducibles for abduction. This holds promise for strengthening the capability of abductive reasoning by adding the feature of automatic preparation of abducibles. Another view point is to use abduction to propose appropriate similarity relations to establish analogical reasoning, which has been reported in this paper. In other words, abduction and analogy are supporting for each other. An ideal implementation of a complementary abduction-analogy system is future research work.

Acknowledgement. We express our special thanks to Professor Katsumi Inoue from National Institute of Informatics, Professor Hidetomo Nabeshima from Yamanashi University and Professor Randy Goebel from Alberta University for their suggestions and fruitful discussions on how to incorporate analogy into abduction. This research was conducted in the Grants-in-Aid for Scientific Research Category C: Supports on Skill Discovery by Rule Abduction and Analogy, Grant No. 24500183.

References

1. Furukawa, K., Inoue, K., Kobayashi, I., Suwa, M.: Discovering knack by abductive reasoning. In: 23rd Congress of JSAI, 1K1-OS8-5 (2009) (in Japanese)
2. Inoue, K., Furukawa, K., Kobayashi, I., Nabeshima, H.: Discovering rules by meta-level abduction. In: De Raedt, L. (ed.) ILP 2009. LNCS, vol. 5989, pp. 49–64. Springer, Heidelberg (2010)
3. Defourneaux, G., Peltier, N.: Analogy and abduction in automated deduction. In: Proceedings of 15th International Joint Conference on Artificial Intelligence (IJCAI-97), vol. 1, pp. 216–225 (1997)
4. Sadohara, K., Haraguchi, M.: Analogical logic program synthesis from examples. In: Lavrač, N., Wrobel, S. (eds.) ECML 1995. LNCS, vol. 912, pp. 232–244. Springer, Heidelberg (1995)
5. Satoh, K.: Translating case-based reasoning into abductive logic programming. In: Proceedings of 12th European Conference on Artificial Intelligence (ECAI 1996), pp. 142–146 (1996)
6. Inoue, K.: Linear resolution for consequence finding. Artif. Intell. **56**(2/3), 301–353 (1992). (Elsevier)
7. Nabeshima, H., Iwanuma, K., Inoue, K.: SOLAR: a consequence finding system for advanced reasoning. In: Cialdea Mayer, M., Pirri, F. (eds.) TABLEAUX 2003. LNCS, vol. 2796, pp. 257–263. Springer, Heidelberg (2003)
8. Muggleton, S., Raedt, L.D.: Inductive logic programming: theory and methods. J. Logic Program. **19/20**, 629–679 (1994). (Elsevier)
9. Haraguchi, M., Arikawa, S.: A formulation of analogical reasoning and its realization. J. Jpn. Soc. Artif. Intell. **1**(1), 132–139 (1986). (in Japanese)
10. Goebel, R.: A sketch of analogy as reasoning with equality hypotheses. In: Jantke, K.P. (ed.) AII 1989. LNCS, vol. 397, pp. 243–253. Springer, Heidelberg (1989)
11. Haraguchi, M.: Towards a mathematical theory of analogy. Bull. Inform. Cybern. **21**(3/4), 29–56 (1985)

Mining Interesting Disjunctive Association Rules from Unfrequent Items

Ines Hilali[1,2], Tao-Yuan Jen[1], Dominique Laurent[1(✉)],
Claudia Marinica[1], and Sadok Ben Yahia[2]

[1] ETIS Laboratory - ENSEA / UCP / CNRS, Cergy-Pontoise, France
[2] Faculty of Sciences of Tunis, University of Tunis El Manar, Tunis, Tunisia
{dlaurent,jen,claudia.marinica}@u-cergy.fr,
ines.hilali@gmail.com, sadok.benyahia@fst.rnu.tn

Abstract. In most approaches to mining association rules, interestingness relies on *frequent* items, i.e., rules are built using items that frequently occur in the transactions. However, in many cases, data sets contain unfrequent items that can reveal useful knowledge that most standard algorithms fail to mine. For example, if items are products, it might be that each of the products p_1 and p_2 does not sell very well (i.e., none of them appears frequently in the transactions) but, that selling products p_1 *or* p_2 is frequent (i.e., transactions containing p_1 *or* p_2 are frequent). Then, assuming that p_1 and p_2 are similar enough with respect to a given similarity measure, the set $\{p_1, p_2\}$ can be considered for mining relevant rules of the form $\{p_1, p_2\} \rightarrow \{p_3, p_4\}$ (assuming that p_3 and p_4 are unfrequent similar products such that $\{p_3, p_4\}$ is frequent), meaning that most of customers buying p_1 or p_2, also buy p_3 or p_4. The goal of our work is to mine association rules of the form $D_1 \rightarrow D_2$ such that (i) D_1 and D_2 are disjoint homogeneous frequent itemsets made up with unfrequent items, and (ii) the support and the confidence of the rule are respectively greater than or equal to given thresholds. The main contributions of this paper towards this goal are to set the formal definitions, properties and algorithms for mining such rules.

Keywords: Data mining · Association rules · Unfrequent items · Similarity measures

1   Introduction

The extraction of association rules is a widely used technique in data mining since it meets the needs of experts in several application fields. Thereby, several studies have focused on *frequent* itemsets mining, i.e., rules are built using items that frequently occur in the transactions. Nevertheless, the application of these patterns is not so attractive in many applications, e.g., intrusion detection, fraud detection, identification of extreme values in data bases, analysis of criminal data, analysis of the genetic confusion from biological data, to cite a few [3,7,10,15].

A. Kawtrakul et al. (Eds.): ISIP 2013, CCIS 421, pp. 84–99, 2014.
DOI: 10.1007/978-3-319-08732-0_7, © Springer International Publishing Switzerland 2014

Indeed, in such situations, a frequent behaviour may not be of an added value for the end user. However, unfrequent events may be more interesting since they may indicate that an unexpected event or exception has occurred. Thus, the analysis has to be carried out in order to study the possible causes of this unusual deviation from normal behaviour. In this respect, unfrequent (or rare) pattern mining is proved to be of real added value [10]. In fact, rare patterns can identify unusual, unexpected and hidden events [2], since they have a very low frequency in the database.

To illustrate such a statement and standing within the market basket analysis, it is common that each of the products p_1 and p_2 does not sell well (i.e., taken alone, none of them appears frequently in the transactions) but, that selling products p_1 *or* p_2 is frequent (i.e., transactions containing p_1 or p_2 are frequent). Additionally, assuming that a similarity measure between products is provided and that products p_1 and p_2 are similar enough, then the set $\{p_1, p_2\}$ can be considered for mining relevant rules of the form $\{p_1, p_2\} \rightarrow \{p_3, p_4\}$ (assuming that p_3 and p_4 are also unfrequent similar products such that $\{p_3, p_4\}$ is frequent). Such a rule shows that most of customers buying p_1 or p_2, also buy p_3 or p_4. In this rule, $\{p_1, p_2\}$ and $\{p_3, p_4\}$ are seen as two different *homogeneous* frequent sets of products.

It is important to mention that, to the best of our knowledge, no previous work has paid attention to mining association rules in which *unfrequent* items are used to build up itemsets meant to be frequent. To address this issue, we measure the frequency of itemsets according to their *disjunctive* support measure [8]. More precisely, we call disjunctive support of an itemset I, or d-support of I for short, the ratio of the number of transactions containing *at least one* element of I over the total number of transactions. Then, I is said to be *disjunctive-frequent* (or d-frequent, for short) if its d-support is greater than or equal to a fixed threshold. It is important to note that, since any super set of a d-frequent itemset is d-frequent as well, we restrict the set of mined d-frequent itemsets to be *minimal* with respect to set inclusion.

Additionally, another worth of mention feature of our approach is our consideration of "homogeneous itemsets". To define this notion, we assume that a similarity measure between items is given, and then, an itemset I is said to be *homogeneous* whenever all possible pairs of items in I have a similarity degree greater than or equal to a given threshold. Thus, the homogeneity can be seen as a semantic interestingness criterion for selecting relevant itemsets, as done in [12]. Indeed, since in our approach, itemsets are assessed through their disjunctive support, an itemset $\{i_1, i_2\}$ is seen as a generalization of i_1 and i_2, in the sense that, based on the definition of the d-support, this set represents a frequent category of items encompassing i_1 and i_2. Therefore, considering the homogeneity avoids the pitfall of considering heterogeneous itemsets, whose "disjunctive semantics" would then be counter intuitive.

In this context, the association rules that we are interested in are of the form $D_1 \rightarrow D_2$ where D_1 and D_2 are disjoint homogeneous and d-frequent itemsets.

Consequently, we redefine the classical support and confidence measures, respectively called d-support and d-confidence, as follows:

– The d-support of a rule $D_1 \rightarrow D_2$ is the number of transactions containing at least one item in D_1 and at least one item in D_2 over the total number of transactions.
– The d-confidence of a rule $D_1 \rightarrow D_2$ is the ratio of the d-support of $D_1 \rightarrow D_2$ over the d-support of D_1.

However, compared to the standard approach to mining association rules, new issues arise when considering d-support and d-confidence. In fact, it turns out that having at hand the d-supports of D_1 and D_2 does *not* imply that the exact retrieval of the d-support as well as the d-confidence of $D_1 \rightarrow D_2$. Thus, assessing the rules in our approach requires to access the data set. Furthermore, owe to the fulfilment of the monotonicity property of the d-frequent itemsets, we focus on minimal itemsets (with respect to set inclusion), in order to produce only rules whose left- and right- hand sides are minimal (with respect to set inclusion).

To sum up, the main contributions of the present paper are twofold: First, we reconsider our previous work in [8] within the context of transactional databases and we provide the necessary definitions and properties used to show the soundness of mining homogeneous association rules built up with unfrequent items, and using a level wise based exploration algorithm. Second, we provide the associated algorithms for each of the following two steps:

1. Mine *minimal and homogeneous d-frequent itemsets*, referred to as MHDIs in what follows.
2. Use the MHDIs to build up and assess association the rules of interest, which are shown to be of the form $D_1 \rightarrow D_2$ where D_1 is an MHDI, D_2 is a homogeneous d-frequent itemset (not necessarily minimal) disjoint from D_1, and whose d-support and d-confidence are above the given thresholds.

The remainder of the paper is organized as follows: In Sect. 2, we give all basic definitions and properties necessary to state and prove the correctness of our algorithms given in Sect. 3. In Sect. 4, we review several approaches dealing with mining techniques using unfrequent items and we compare these approaches with our work. In Sect. 5, we briefly recall our contributions and we sketch several issues for future work.

2   Formalism and Basic Properties

In this section we give the necessary definitions and properties on which our algorithms rely. We define the notions of disjunctive support of an itemset and of a rule, the disjunctive confidence of a rule, and what we call an homogeneous itemset. These definitions are then used in some basic properties that are necessary to show the correctness of the algorithms to be given in the next section.

2.1 Support and Confidence

We assume a set $\mathcal{I}$ of items that occur in a transaction table Δ whose rows are called transactions. A transaction is a pair (TID, I) where TID is a transaction identifier and I a subset of $\mathcal{I}$, also called an itemset. We borrow from [8] the notion of disjunctive support of an itemset D, that we define as follows.

Definition 1. *For every itemset D, the disjunctive support of D, or d-support of D for short, denoted by d-sup(D), is the ratio*

$$d\text{-}sup(D) = \frac{|\{(\text{TID}, I) \in \Delta \mid I \cap D \neq \emptyset\}|}{|\Delta|}.$$

Given a support threshold σ, D is said to be disjunctive-frequent, *or d-frequent for short, if d-sup$(D) \geq \sigma$.*

We emphasize that Definition 1 implies that the notion of d-support differs from that of support as defined in [1]. Indeed, given an itemset I, the support of I is computed based on the number of transactions containing *all* items in I.

To illustrate our approach, we consider the following example that will be used as a running example throughout the paper.

Example 1. Let $\mathcal{I} = \{bergerac, cheverny, montlouis, milk, scallop, oyster, salad\}$ be a set of items where *bergerac*, *cheverny* and *montlouis* are names of French wines. We assume the set of transactions Δ as shown in Table 1. To simplify, for every $j = 1, \ldots, 7$, the transaction with TID equal to j is denoted by t_j; for example, t_1 refers to the first transaction in Δ, that is $(1, \{bergerac, milk, scallop\})$.

Table 1. The set of transactions Δ of the running example.

TID	I
1	Bergerac, milk, scallop
2	Cheverny, milk, scallop
3	Scallop
4	Bergerac, milk, oyster
5	Montlouis, oysyer
6	Salad
7	Montlouis

Denoting by $sup(D)$ the support of an itemset D as defined in [1], for $D = \{cheverny, milk\}$ and $D' = \{oyster, milk\}$, we have:

- $sup(D) = \frac{|\{t_2\}|}{7} = \frac{1}{7} = 14.3\,\%$ and $d\text{-}sup(D) = \frac{|\{t_1, t_2, t_4\}|}{7} = \frac{3}{7} = 42\,\%$
- $sup(D') = \frac{|\{t_4\}|}{7} = \frac{1}{7} = 14.3\,\%$ and $d\text{-}sup(D') = \frac{|\{t_1, t_2, t_4, t_5\}|}{7} = \frac{4}{7} = 57.1\,\%$

For a threshold $\sigma = 50\%$, D and D' are not frequent, D is not d-frequent and D' is d-frequent. We also note that no item is frequent with respect to σ.   □

It is easy to see that the disjunctive support measure is monotonic with respect to set inclusion, in other words the following proposition holds.

Proposition 1. *For all itemsets D_1 and D_2, if $D_1 \subseteq D_2$ then d-sup$(D_1) \leq$ d-sup(D_2).*

Proposition 1 implies that if $D_1 \subseteq D_2$ and if D_2 is *not* d-frequent, then D_1 can not be d-frequent. Hence, (i) minimal d-frequent itemsets can be mined using a level wise algorithm such as Apriori, and (ii) knowing the minimal d-frequent itemsets allows for knowing *all* d-frequent itemsets (but not their d-supports). We now define disjunctive support and confidence of association rules.

Definition 2. *Let D_1 and D_2 be two itemsets. The* disjunctive support, *or d-support for short, of $D_1 \rightarrow D_2$, denoted by d-sup$(D_1 \rightarrow D_2)$, is the ratio*

$$d\text{-}sup(D_1 \rightarrow D_2) = \frac{|\{(\text{TID}, I) \in \Delta \mid (I \cap D_1 \neq \emptyset) \wedge (I \cap D_2 \neq \emptyset)\}|}{|\Delta|}.$$

Given a support threshold σ, $D_1 \rightarrow D_2$ is said to be disjunctive-frequent, *or d-frequent for short, if d-sup$(D_1 \rightarrow D_2) \geq \sigma$.*

The disjunctive confidence, *or d-confidence for short, of $D_1 \rightarrow D_2$, denoted by d-conf$(D_1 \rightarrow D_2)$, is the ratio*

$$d\text{-}conf(D_1 \rightarrow D_2) = \frac{d\text{-}sup(D_1 \rightarrow D_2)}{d\text{-}sup(D_1)}.$$

Example 2. In the context of Example 1, for $D_1 = \{bergerac, montlouis\}$ and $D_2 = \{scallop, oyster\}$, we have that:

- $d\text{-}sup(D_1) = \frac{|\{t_1, t_4, t_5, t_7\}|}{7} = 57.1\%$, $d\text{-}sup(D_2) = \frac{|\{t_1, t_2, t_3, t_4, t_5\}|}{7} = 71.4\%$,
- $d\text{-}sup(D_1 \rightarrow D_2) = d\text{-}sup(D_2 \rightarrow D_1) = \frac{|\{t_1, t_4, t_5\}|}{7} = 42.8\%$.

As a consequence, for a support threshold $\sigma = 50\%$, the two rules $D_1 \rightarrow D_2$ and $D_2 \rightarrow D_1$ are not frequent. On the other hand, we have $d\text{-}conf(D_1 \rightarrow D_2) = \frac{42.8}{57.1} = 75\%$ and $d\text{-}conf(D_2 \rightarrow D_1) = \frac{42.8}{71.4} = 60\%$.   □

It is important to note from Definition 2 that the notions of d-support and d-confidence of an association rule carry similar semantics as standard support and confidence for association rules. Indeed:

- The d-support of $D_1 \rightarrow D_2$ is the probability that a transaction contains at least one item in D_1 and at least one item in D_2 (recalling that the standard support of $D_1 \rightarrow D_2$ can be seen as the probability that a transaction contains all items in D_1 and all items in D_2).

– The d-confidence of $D_1 \to D_2$ is the conditional probability that a transaction contains at least one item in D_1 and at least one item in D_2, knowing that it contains at least one item in D_1 (recalling that the standard confidence of $D_1 \to D_2$ can be seen as the conditional probability that a transaction contains all items in D_1 and all items in D_2 knowing that it contains all items in D_1).

The following proposition states basic properties of d-support and d-confidence.

Proposition 2. *For all itemsets D_1, D_2 and D, we have:*

1. $d\text{-}sup(D_1 \to D_2) \leq d\text{-}sup(D_j)$ *for* $j = 1, 2$
2. $d\text{-}sup(D_1 \to D_2) \leq d\text{-}sup((D_1 \cup D) \to D_2)$
3. $d\text{-}sup(D_1 \to D_2) \leq d\text{-}sup(D_1 \to (D_2 \cup D))$
4. $d\text{-}conf(D_1 \to D_2) \leq d\text{-}conf(D_1 \to (D_2 \cup D))$
5. $d\text{-}sup(D_1 \to D_2) = d\text{-}sup(D_1 \to (D_2 \cup D)) \iff d\text{-}conf(D_1 \to D_2) = d\text{-}conf(D_1 \to (D_2 \cup D))$

2.2 Homogeneous Itemsets

As already mentioned, interestingness of itemsets is measured based not only on their d-frequency, but also on their *homogeneity*. Homogeneity of itemsets is defined using a *similarity measure*, that we denote by *sim*. We recall in this respect that similarity measures have been considered in data mining since they allow taking into account semantic aspects in the processing ([12,13,16]).

In this work, we consider the similarity measure defined in [16], called *Total Relatedness*. Assuming a taxonomy over the items, this measure is composed of two other partial similarity measures, called *Highest-Level Relatedness* and *Node Separation Relatedness*, and defined as follows, where i and i' are distinct items in $\mathcal{I}$:

– The Highest-Level Relatedness of i and i', denoted by $HR(i, i')$, is the level of the highest-level node of the path in the taxonomy connecting i and i'.
– The Node Separation Relatedness of i and i' ($i \neq i'$), denoted by $NSR(i, i')$, is the number of nodes in the path connecting i and i' in the taxonomy.

If k is the depth of the taxonomy, the *Total Relatedness measure* is defined by:

$$sim(i, i') = \frac{1 + HR(i, i')}{k * NSR(i, i')}.$$

Example 3. In the context of Example 1, a taxonomy over the items in $\mathcal{I}$ is shown in Fig. 1. In this setting, we have:

– $HR(bergerac, montlouis) = 1$ and $HR(milk, scallop) = 0$,
– $NSR(bergerac, montlouis) = 1$ and $NSR(milk, scallop) = 3$.

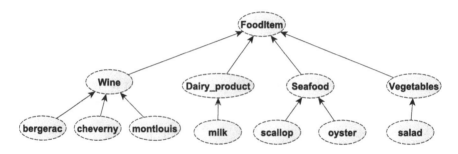

Fig. 1. Taxonomical organization of the items of Example 1

Therefore, according to the definition of sim given above, we have:
$sim(bergerac, montlouis) = \frac{2}{2} = 1$ and $sim(milk, scallop) = \frac{1}{6}$.   □

The notion of homogeneous itemset is defined as follows.

Definition 3. *Let h be a value in the range of the similarity measure sim. An itemset I is said to be* homogeneous *with respect to h if $\min_{i,i' \in I}(sim(i, i')) \geq h$.*

Referring back to Example 3 and considering a similarity threshold $h = 1$, $\{bergerac, montlouis\}$ is homogeneous, whereas $\{milk, scallop\}$ is not.

Since for all itemsets I_1 and I_2 such that $I_1 \subseteq I_2$, $\min_{i,i' \in I_1}(sim(i, i')) \geq \min_{i,i' \in I_2}(sim(i, i'))$ holds, it is easy to see that the following holds.

Proposition 3. *For all itemsets I_1 and I_2 such that $I_1 \subseteq I_2$, if I_2 is homogeneous then I_1 is homogeneous as well.*

In what follows, we call MHDI any *minimal homogeneous d-frequent itemset*, and we consider the problem of mining *all* MHDIs from Δ. An important consequence of Propositions 1 and 3 is that MHDIs can be mined using a level wise algorithm such as Apriori [1].

As another remark concerning homogeneous itemsets, deciding whether an itemset I is homogeneous or not clearly requires a number of tests in $O(|I|^2)$. However, if I is known to be homogeneous, checking whether $I \cup \{i\}$ (where i is an item not in I) is homogeneous only requires to check whether $\min_{i' \in I}(sim(i, i'))$ is greater than or equal to h. Therefore, in this case, checking whether $I \cup \{i\}$ is homogeneous is in $O(|I|)$.

The previous remark is of particular interest in the forthcoming Algorithm 2, where we assume that, for every MHDI D, the set $H(D)$ of all unfrequent items i such that $D \cup \{i\}$ is homogeneous has been computed beforehand.

3 Algorithms

In this section, we present the two algorithms that implement our approach: the first algorithm allows for the computation of all MHDIs whereas the second one allows for the computation of all interesting rules. Before going into the details of these algorithms, we note the following points regarding computations:

1. To avoid computation redundancies when generating candidates, we assume that a total ordering $\prec_{\mathcal{I}}$ over $\mathcal{I}$ is given and that the items of all itemsets are listed according to this ordering.
2. To check whether an itemset I is homogeneous, we assume that all similarity degrees between unfrequent items have been computed and stored. Although we do not provide details regarding this point, we shall see that it can be achieved during the processing of the first algorithm given below.
3. As earlier mentioned, we assume that for every MHDI D, the set $H(D)$ of all unfrequent items i such that $D \cup \{i\}$ is homogeneous has been computed and stored.

3.1   MHDI Computation

As argued in the previous section, MHDIs are mined using a level wise algorithm similar to Apriori [1]. This task is achieved by Algorithm 1 where the set of candidates, denoted by hom_cand, is generated by joining the elements of $unfreq\_hom_{k_1}$, i.e., the non d-frequent homogeneous itemsets of size $k - 1$ and by pruning the obtained set of itemsets. We note that this assumes that the items of itemsets are listed according to the ordering $\prec_{\mathcal{I}}$.

The main difference with the standard algorithm Apriori is that the homogeneity criterion has to be taken into account, which is achieved line 11. Indeed, if all subsets of $D_1 \cup D_2$ of cardinality $k - 1$ are homogeneous, then by Proposition 3, so is $\{i_1^{k-1}, i_2^{k-1}\}$. Therefore, for all i_1 and i_2 in $D_1 \cup D_2$, we have $sim(i_1, i_2) \geq h$, meaning that $D_1 \cup D_2$ is homogeneous.

The correctness of Algorithm 1 can be shown as in [8], where this was done in the context of relational disjunctive queries with no homogeneity criterion. We simply note that, in our context, candidates are selected for the next step if they are non d-frequent and homogeneous. Thus, every non selected itemset is d-frequent *or* not homogeneous. Since the itemsets in hom_cand are homogeneous, non selected itemsets for the next step are homogeneous and d-frequent. Moreover, these itemsets are also minimal with respect to set inclusion since their subsets have been previously considered as non d-frequent itemsets. Consequently Algorithm 1 correctly computes all MHDIs.

We now argue that the complexity of Algorithm 1 is similar to that of the standard Apriori algorithm [1]. To see this, we express the complexity of Algorithm 1 in terms of the number of scans of the data set Δ, as for the standard Apriori algorithm. In this case, since Algorithm 1 performs a scan of Δ at each level of the lattice built up with all unfrequent items (see lines 16–19), we obtain that the complexity of Algorithm 1 is linear in the number of unfrequent items (in the same way as the complexity of the standard Apriori algorithm is shown to be linear in the number of frequent items). Hence, similarly to the standard Apriori algorithm, the complexity of Algorithm 1 is in $O(|\mathcal{I}|)$ (considering the worst case when no item is frequent).

Regarding this complexity result, we emphasize that restricting the mined itemsets to be homogeneous has no impact on the complexity of Algorithm 1. We note in this respect that in Algorithm 1 some details have been omitted for

---

Algorithm 1. Computation of MHDIs

Input: Database Δ, the d-support threshold σ, the similarity threshold h
Output: The set $MHDI(\Delta)$ of all MHDIs
1: // Scan Δ to compute the set of all unfrequent items
2: $unfreq\_hom_1 = \{i \in \mathcal{I} \mid d\text{-}sup(i) < \sigma\}$
3: $MHDI(\Delta) = \emptyset$
4: $k = 2$
5: **while** $unfreq\_hom_{k-1} \neq \emptyset$ **do**
6:    $hom\_cand = \emptyset$
7:    // Candidate generation
8:    **for all** D_1 and D_2 in $unfreq\_hom_{k-1}$ **do**
9:       // $D_1 = \{i_1^1, \ldots, i_1^{k-1}\}, D_2 = \{i_2^1, \ldots, i_2^{k-1}\}$
10:       **if** $i_1^1 = i_2^1$ and ... and $i_1^{k-2} = i_2^{k-2}$ and $i_1^{k-1} \prec_\mathcal{I} i_2^{k-1}$ **then**
11:          **if** all subsets of $(D_1 \cup D_2)$ of cardinality $k-1$ are in $unfreq\_hom_{k-1}$ **then**
12:             $hom\_cand = hom\_cand \cup \{(D1 \cup D_2)\}$
13:    **for all** D in hom_cand **do**
14:       $d\text{-}sup(D) = 0$
15:    // Scan of Δ to compute the d-supports of all D in hom_cand
16:    **for all** (TID, I) in Δ **do**
17:       **for all** D in hom_cand **do**
18:          **if** $D \cap I \neq \emptyset$ **then**
19:             $d\text{-}sup(D) = d\text{-}sup(D) + 1$
20:    $unfreq\_hom_k = \{D \in hom\_cand \mid d\text{-}sup(D) < \sigma\}$
21:    $MHDI(\Delta) = MHDI(\Delta) \cup \{D \in hom\_cand \mid d\text{-}sup(D) \geq \sigma\}$
22:    $k = k + 1$
23: **return** $MHDI(\Delta)$

---

the sake of simplification. In particular, the test line 11 is not necessary when $k = 2$ (because it is always satisfied in this case). However, for $k = 2$, when considering a candidate itemset $D = \{i_1^1, i_2^1\}$, checking whether D is homogeneous amounts to check whether $sim(i_1^1, i_2^1) \geq h$, which in turn, requires to compute $sim(i_1^1, i_2^1)$. This computation does not impact the complexity result mentioned above because similarity is computed based on the given ontology and similarity measure, but *not* based on the data set Δ. We also mention that these similarity results are assumed to be stored in a matrix so as to efficiently compute the sets $H(D)$ for every MHDI D, and other similarity measures needed when running Algorithm 2 to be given next.

The following example illustrates how Algorithm 1 works in the context of our running example.

Example 4. Referring to the data set Δ shown in Table 1, and considering the support threshold $\sigma = 50\%$ and the similarity threshold $h = 1$, Algorithm 1 performs the following steps:

– First, the computation of $unfreq\_hom_1$ line 2 returns $\mathcal{I}$, because, as mentioned in Example 1, no item in $\mathcal{I}$ is frequent.
– For $k = 2$, all possible pairs of items are considered in the loop lines 8–12, and for all distinct i, i' in $\mathcal{I}$, $sim(i, i')$ is computed and stored. Moreover, the

d-supports of the homogeneous pairs are computed through the scan lines 16–19: we obtain that the homogeneous d-frequent itemsets of cardinality 2 are $\{bergerac, montlouis\}$ and $\{scallop, oyster\}$.

Therefore $unfreq\_hom_2$ contains the two itemsets: $\{bergerac, cheverny\}$ and $\{cheverny, montlouis\}$ (since the other unfrequent itemsets of cardinality 2 are not homogeneous).

– For $k = 3$, no candidates are generated line 10, and so the main iteration lines 5–22 stops when k is set to 4, line 22.

Hence, $\{bergerac, montlouis\}$ and $\{scallop, oyster\}$ are the two MHDIs returned by Algorithm 1.   □

3.2   From MHDIs to Interesting Association Rules

The output of Algorithm 1 is used to build and assess candidate rules in order to produce the final result. However, in our approach, and contrary to the standard case, the assessment of these candidate rules requires to scan the dataset. This is so because, knowing the d-supports of D_1 and D_2 does not imply that $d\text{-}sup(D_1 \to D_2)$ can be computed without scanning the data.

Moreover, according to Proposition 2(1), the d-support of a rule $D_1 \to D_2$ is less than the d-supports of D_1 and D_2. Hence, considering only rules $D_1 \to D_2$ where D_1 and D_2 are MHDIs is likely to produce a very limited number of rules. On the other hand, Proposition 2(1-2) states that the d-support of a rule $D_1 \to D_2$ increases when one of the itemsets D_1 or D_2 is enlarged. This is why we look for association rules of the form $D_1 \to D_2$ where D_1 and D_2 are homogeneous d-frequent itemsets, that might not be MHDIs. Moreover, we naturally require that these sets be "as small as possible" because it is well known that in practice, rules with too many members in their left- and/or right-hand sides are difficult to understand by users.

We now emphasize that, by Proposition 2(2-4), enlarging the right hand side of a rule increases the d-support *and* the d-confidence of the rule, whereas enlarging the left hand side increases the d-support, but not always the d-confidence. In fact, we claim that enlarging the left hand sides of rules is not relevant in our approach. To see this, denoting by $T(D)$ be the set of transactions TID,I in Δ such that $(I \cap D) \neq \emptyset$, we notice that a rule $D_1 \to D_2$ whose confidence is 1, that is for which $d\text{-}sup(D_1 \to D_2) = d\text{-}sup(D_1)$, satisfies $T(D_1) \subseteq T(D_2)$. Thus, improving the d-confidence of a rule $D_1 \to D_2$ whose d-confidence is not 1 tends to make $T(D_1)$ a subset of $T(D_2)$. This can not be achieved by enlarging D_1 because enlarging D_1 entails that $T(D_1)$ is also enlarged.

Based on the previous remarks, the rules we are looking for are of the form $D_1 \to D_2$, such that, given thresholds σ, γ and h:

1. D_1 is an MHDI and D_2 is a homogeneous d-frequent itemset;
2. D_1 and D_2 are disjoint;
3. $d\text{-}sup(D_1 \to D_2) \geq \sigma$ and $d\text{-}conf(D_1 \to D_2) \geq \gamma$;
4. for every rule $D_1 \to D_2$ satisfying the three items above, and for every $D \subset D_2$, the rule $D_1 \to D$ does *not* satisfy all three items above.

Algorithm 2. The computation of all interesting association rules

---

Input: Δ, the set $MHDI(\Delta)$ of all MHDIs, the d-support threshold σ, the d-confidence threshold γ, the similarity threshold h
Output: The set $Result$ of all interesting association rules

    // **Step 1 :** level $k = 0$

1: $C = \emptyset$
2: **for all** (D_1, D_2) in $MHDI(\Delta) \times MHDI(\Delta)$ **do**
3:    **if** $D_1 \cap D_2 = \emptyset$ **then**
4:      $C = C \cup \{(D_1, D_2, \emptyset, d\text{-}sup(D_1), 0, 0)\}$
5: $Result = \emptyset$
6: Scan Δ to compute S-new $= d\text{-}sup(D_1 \to D_2)$ of rules in C
7: **for all** $c = (D_1, D_2, \emptyset, s, 0, \text{S-new})$ in C **do**
8:    **if** S-new $\geq \sigma$ and $d\text{-}conf(D_1 \to D_2) \geq \gamma$ **then**
9:      $Result = Result \cup \{D_1 \to D_2\}$
10:     $C = C \setminus \{c\}$
11:    **else**
12:      **if** S-new $=$ S-old **then**
13:        $C = C \setminus \{c\}$
14: C-old $= C$

    // **Step 2:** levels k with $k > 0$

15: **while** C-old $\neq \emptyset$ **do**
16:   C-new $= \emptyset$
17:   **for all** $c = (D_1, D_2, E, s, \text{S-old}, \text{S-new})$ in C-old **do**
18:     **for all** i in $(H(D_2) \setminus (D_2 \cup E \cup D_1))$, and $\max_{\mathcal{I}}(E) \prec_{\mathcal{I}} i$ **do**
19:       **if** $(D_2 \cup E \cup \{i\})$ is homogeneous **then**
20:         $c' = (D_1, D_2, E \cup \{i\}, s, \text{S-new}, 0)$
21:         C-new $=$ C-new $\cup \{c'\}$
22:   Scan Δ to compute S-new $= d\text{-}sup(D_1 \to D_2 \cup E \cup \{i\})$ of rules in C-new
23:   **for all** $c = (D_1, D_2, E \cup \{i\}, s, \text{S-old}, \text{S-new})$ in C-new **do**
24:     **if** S-new $\geq \sigma$ and $d\text{-}conf(D_1 \to D_2 \cup E \cup \{i\}) \geq \gamma$ **then**
25:       $Result = Result \cup \{D_1 \to D_2 \cup E \cup \{i\}\}$
26:       C-new $=$ C-new $\setminus \{c\}$
27:     **else**
28:       **if** S-old $=$ S-new **then**
29:         C-new $=$ C-new $\setminus \{c\}$
30:   C-old $=$ C-new
31: Delete from $Result$ all rules $D_1 \to D_2 \cup E$ such that $Result$ contains $D_1 \to D_2' \cup E'$ with $D_2' \cup E' \subset D_2 \cup E$
32: **return** $Result$

Calling these rules *interesting association rules*, we provide next an algorithm for mining them. Before doing so, we give examples of interesting rules.

Example 5. In the context of our running example, we recall from Example 4 that we have $MHDI(\Delta) = \{D_1, D_2\}$ where $D_1 = \{bergerac, montlouis\}$ and $D_2 = \{scallop, oyster\}$. Thus, the only rules to be considered first are $D_1 \to D_2$

and $D_2 \to D_1$. However, as seen in Example 2, none of these rules is d-frequent, since their d-support has been shown to be less than 50 %. Consequently, these rules cannot be interesting.

As suggested just above, in order to get interesting rules we extend the right-hand sides of $D_1 \to D_2$ and $D_2 \to D_1$, in order to satisfy the four previous conditions for a confidence threshold $\gamma = 75$ %.

- Regarding the rule $D_1 \to D_2$, we have to extend D_2 into a homogeneous d-frequent itemset D_2', which is not possible because for every item i in $\mathcal{I}$ but not in $D_1 \cup D_2$, $(D_2 \cup \{i\})$ is not homogeneous.
- Considering now $D_2 \to D_1$, we notice that the item *cheverny* is the only item in $\mathcal{I}$ such that $D_1' = (D_1 \cup \{cheverny\})$ is homogeneous. Moreover:
  - $d\text{-}sup(D_2 \to D_1') = \frac{|\{t_1, t_2, t_4, t_5\}|}{7} = 57.1$ %, and
  - $d\text{-}conf(D_2 \to D_1') = \frac{57.1}{71.4} = 80$ %.

  Therefore $D_2 \to D_1'$ satisfies the first three conditions above, and as it can be seen that this rule also satisfies the last condition, $D_2 \to D_1'$ is an interesting association rule. □

3.3 An Algorithm for Mining all Interesting Association Rules

Interesting association rules are mined according to Algorithm 2 in which a 6-tuple $(D_1, D_2, E, s, \text{S-old}, \text{S-new})$ represents the rule $D_1 \to (D_2 \cup E)$ where:

- D_1 and D_2 are MHDIs, and E is an itemset containing unfrequent items,
- s is the d-support of D_1 (s is known from the run of Algorithm 1),
- S-old $= 0$ if $E = \emptyset$, and otherwise, S-old is the d-support of a rule of the form $D_1 \to (D_2 \cup (E \setminus \{i\}))$ from the previous iteration,
- S-new is the d-support of $D_1 \to (D_2 \cup E)$.

We now discuss the steps of Algorithm 2. In Step 1, we first filter out all pairs of MHDIs (D_1, D_2) where D_1 and D_2 are not disjoint, and the 6-tuples of all remaining potentially interesting rules $D_1 \to D_2$ are put in the set of candidates (line 4). The supports of these rules are then computed through a scan of Δ (line 6). All candidates whose d-support and d-confidence are respectively greater than or equal to their corresponding threshold are added to the result set *Result* (line 9) and will not be considered in the next step, due to our minimal requirement (line 10). For all other candidates, the test line 12 discards the rule if its d-support is 0, since this means that no transaction d-supports the rule.

The iteration in Step 2 enlarges the right hand sides of the rules in a level wise manner as follows: new candidates are generated by adding one item to the set E thus producing the candidate rule $D_1 \to (D_2 \cup E \cup \{i\})$ from the rule $D_1 \to (D_2 \cup E)$. We note that in order to avoid computational redundancies, the ordering $\prec_{\mathcal{I}}$ is used (see line 18). We also emphasize here that we assume that for every D in $MHDI(\Delta)$, the set $H(D)$ has been already computed. Under this hypothesis, line 18, the item i is chosen in $H(D_2)$, because otherwise, $D_2 \cup E \cup \{i\}$ cannot be homogeneous. However, it is still necessary to check whether $D_2 \cup E \cup \{i\}$ is homogeneous, which is done line 19.

Lines 18 to 30 show a processing similar to that of lines 3 to 14 of Step 1, that is: new candidates are generated (lines 17–21) and Δ is scanned in order to compute the current d-supports stored in S-new (line 22). Then, these new candidates are processed according to the fact that they represent or not an interesting rule (lines 23–29). We notice that candidates such that S-new = S-old (line 28) are discarded because Proposition 2(5) shows that, in this case, adding i to the right hand side does not change the d-support and the d-confidence. Therefore, the rule $D_1 \rightarrow (D_2 \cup E \cup \{i\})$ has not to be considered in the next iterations. On the other hand, minimality of the right hand sides of rules is guaranteed line 31, where non minimal rules are discarded. As a consequence, it turns out that Algorithm 2 computes the expected set of all interesting association rules.

We now turn to the study of the complexity of Algorithm 2, which we express in terms of the number of scans of the data set, as done for Algorithm 1. As previously mentioned, in Algorithm 2 candidate rules are generated in a level wise manner by adding one item to the right hand sides of rules, and at each level, the supports and confidences of these candidate rules are computed through one scan of Δ. Therefore, the complexity of Algorithm 2 is the same as that of Algorithm 1, that is in $O(|\mathcal{I}|)$. We also note that, since only items i in $H(D_2)$ are considered to enlarge $D_2 \cup E$, the test of homogeneity line 19, which uses the similarity matrix constructed in Algorithm 1 (for $k = 2$ as previously explained), is linear in the size of E. In other words, the complexity of this test is linear in less than the size of $\mathcal{I}$, even in the worst case.

4   Related Work

Whereas most approaches in data mining are interested in extracting frequent patterns, mining unfrequent or rare patterns (association rules or itemsets) has attracted research efforts these last years [10]. According to these work, rare patterns do not often occur, and are relevant if their elements are strongly correlated. Mining abnormal symptoms in medical applications is a standard example of such patterns. However, it is important to note that, whatever the data set in which these patterns are mined, considering these low-support and high-confidence rules raises major difficulties when using standard association rule mining approaches.

In order to address this issue, some approaches propose to consider the frequency as a relative measure rather than an absolute one, since the items differ from one to another by nature. For example, buying a luxe item is an action much less frequent than buying milk, and so, the corresponding frequencies cannot be interpreted in the same way. In [11], the MSapriori Algorithm has been introduced to mine the absolute unfrequent items by assigning different minimum support thresholds to different items. In [17,20], instead of using different thresholds, a weighted support measurement is used to offer different viewpoints to items. Hence users can assign weights according to their need and find valuable unfrequent patterns. One critical point when applying the previous methods is to assign adequate minimum support thresholds and/or weights to different items. This task becomes even unfeasible when considering a large number of items. This is why, the relative support measure was proposed in [24].

Although relevant patterns can be mined using these approaches, it turns out that in most cases, very large numbers of candidate itemsets are generated, as in the standard case when the thresholds are set to be very low. Several propositions have been introduced to tackle this issue. The proposition in [18,19] is to find rules directly form their confidence. Although, confidence does not have a downward closure property, the authors use a confidence-based pruning in their rule generation. In this approach, high-confidence and low-support association rules of the form $I \rightarrow i$, where I is an itemset and i is an item, are mined without generating unnecessary low-support itemsets. Other work propose to mine highly correlated patterns using appropriate measures, such as h-confidence [21,22] or Bond [4,23]; relationships between these measures are studied in [14].

It is important to note that most approaches to mining rare association rules concentrate on *conjunctive* patterns built up using unfrequent or frequent items. One main risk when considering conjunctions of unfrequent items is that these itemsets have a very low support, and thus, it is difficult to distinguished such patterns from noisy data. This issue has been investigated in [9] through the notion of exception rule.

As opposed to these approaches, our work is based on *disjunction* to build frequent itemsets, and considers a similarity measure as an additional criterion. We note that it has been shown in [4,23] that the disjunctive form of patterns can be derived from the correlated patterns, using the technique in [5]. However, since the correlated patterns are generated from frequent items, we can not use these results in our approach, where we consider unfrequent items.

We notice that in [6], the authors consider a taxonomy to mine frequent itemsets built up with items from the same level in the taxonomy. However, our approach basically differs from this work because in [6], only frequent items are considered (whereas we consider unfrequent items) and the support threshold is changed according to the level in the taxonomy (whereas we do not change the support threshold during the mining process).

Moreover, the frequent disjunctive itemsets that are mined in our work are built up according to the given taxonomy, but may be different from the concepts defined by this taxonomy. Indeed, in our approach, the taxonomy is used to assess the homogeneity of disjunctive itemsets, according to a given similarity threshold. As a consequence, it is possible that a given homogeneous frequent disjunctive itemset does not "match" existing concepts in the taxonomy, although representing a relevant set of items. We argue that such itemsets can be used to reorganize the ontology, according to the content of the data set and to the similarity threshold chosen by the user (this issue will be investigated in our future work). Hence, it should be clear that the way we use the taxonomy in our approach is radically different from the one in [6].

5   Concluding Remarks

In this paper, we have proposed an approach to mine association rule involving unfrequent items. Unfrequent items are grouped in itemsets to produce frequent itemsets according to the *disjunctive* support measure. In order to produce rules as "understandable" as possible, disjunctive frequent itemsets have been restricted to be minimal with respect to set inclusion, and a homogeneity criterion has been considered for itemsets. We have shown that in this setting, disjunctive frequent itemsets can be mined using a standard level wise algorithm. However, it has also been argued that computing interesting rules in this approach requires further scans of the data set. These scans have been shown to be processed in a level wise manner so as to produce all interesting rules.

We are currently implementing our algorithms to assess their efficiency and their relevancy. To this end, we intend to consider synthetic and real data sets, so as to provide experiments as complete as possible. Regarding further research issues in the context of this work, we mention that considering homogeneous itemsets allows for further investigation. Indeed, homogeneity allows to define groups of unfrequent items, seen as concepts among which rules are to be mined. It seems that the interesting rules considered in this paper are closely related to these rules between concepts. We plan to investigate this issue in the future.

References

1. Agrawal, R., Mannila, H., Srikant, R., Toivonen, R., Verkamo, A.I.: Fast discovery of association rules. In: Advances in Knowledge Discovery and Data Mining, pp. 309–328. AAAI-MIT Press (1996)
2. Berberidis, C., Vlahavas, I.P.: Detection and prediction of rare events in transaction databases. Int. J. Artif. Intell. Tools **16**(5), 829–848 (2007)
3. Booker, Q.E.: Improving identity resolution in criminal justice data: an application of NORA and SUDA. J. Inform. Assur. Secur. **4**, 403–411 (2009)
4. Bouasker, S., Hamrouni, T., Ben Yahia, S.: New exact concise representation of rare correlated patterns: application to intrusion detection. In: Tan, P.-N., Chawla, S., Ho, C.K., Bailey, J. (eds.) PAKDD 2012, Part II. LNCS, vol. 7302, pp. 61–72. Springer, Heidelberg (2012)
5. Hamrouni, T., Ben Yahia, S.: Generalization of association rules through disjunction. Ann. Math. Artif. Intell. **59**(2), 201–222 (2010)
6. Han, J., Fu, Y.: Discovery of multiple-level association rules from large databases. In: PVLDB, pp. 420–431 (1995)
7. He, Z., Xu, X.: FP-OUTLIER: frequent pattern based outlier detection. Comput. Sci. Inf. Syst. **2**(1), 103–118 (2005)
8. Hilali-Jaghdam, I., Jen, T.-Y., Laurent, D., Ben Yahia, S.: Mining frequent disjunctive selection queries. In: Hameurlain, A., Liddle, S.W., Schewe, K.-D., Zhou, X. (eds.) DEXA 2011, Part II. LNCS, vol. 6861, pp. 90–96. Springer, Heidelberg (2011)
9. Hussain, F., Liu, H., Suzuki, E., Lu, H.: Exception rule mining with a relative interestingness measure. In: Terano, T., Liu, H., Chen, A.L.P. (eds.) PAKDD 2000. LNCS, vol. 1805, pp. 86–97. Springer, Heidelberg (2000)

10. Koh, Y.S., Roundtree, N.: Rare Association Rule Mining and Knowledge Discovery: Technologies for Infrequent and Critical Event Detection. IGI Global, Hershey (2010)
11. Liu, B., Hsu, W., Ma, Y.: Mining association rules with multiple minimum supports. In: ACM International Conference on Knowledge Discovery and Data Mining, SIGKDD, pp. 337–341. ACM (1999)
12. Marinica, C., Guillet, F.: Knowledge-based interactive postmining of association rules using ontologies. IEEE Trans. Knowl. Data Eng. **22**(6), 784–797 (2010)
13. Natarajan, R., Shekar, B.: A relatedness-based data-driven approach to determination of interestingness of association rules. In: ACM Symposium on Applied Computing (SAC), pp. 551–552. ACM (2005)
14. Omiecinski, E.R.: Alternative interest measures for mining associations in databases. IEEE Trans. Knowl. Data Eng. **15**(1), 57–69 (2003)
15. Romero, C., Romero, J.R., Luna, J.M., Ventura, S.: Mining rare association rules from e-learning data. In: Proceedings of the 3rd International Conference on Educational Data Mining (EDM 2010), Pittsburgh, PA, USA, pp. 171–180 (2010)
16. Shekar, B., Natarajan, R.: A framework for evaluating knowledge-based interestingness of association rules. Fuzzy Optim. Decis. Making **3**, 157–185 (2004)
17. Tao, F., Murtagh, F., Farid, M.: Weighted association rule mining using weighted support and significance framework. In: ACM International Conference on Knowledge Discovery and Data Mining, SIGKDD, pp. 661–666. ACM (2003)
18. Wang, K., He, Y., Cheung, D.M.: Mining confident rules without support requirement. In: ACM International Conference on Information and Knowledge Management, CIKM, pp. 89–96. ACM (2001)
19. Wang, K., Zhou, S., He, Y.: Growing decision trees on support-less association rules. In: ACM International Conference on Knowledge Discovery and Data Mining, SIGKDD, pp. 265–269. ACM (2000)
20. Wang, W., Yang, J., Yu, P.S.: Efficient mining of weighted association rules (WAR). In: ACM International Conference on Knowledge Discovery and Data Mining, SIGKDD, pp. 270–274. ACM (2000)
21. Xiong, H., Tan, P.N., Koumar, V.: Mining strong affinity association patterns in data sets with skewed support distribution. In: IEEE ICDM, pp. 387–394. ACM (2003)
22. Xiong, H., Tan, P.N., Koumar, V.: Hyperclique pattern discovery. Data Min. Knowl. Discov **13**(2), 219–242 (2006)
23. Younes, N.B., Hamrouni, T., Ben Yahia, S.: Bridging conjunctive and disjunctive search spaces for mining a new concise and exact representation of correlated patterns. In: Pfahringer, B., Holmes, G., Hoffmann, A. (eds.) DS 2010. LNCS, vol. 6332, pp. 189–204. Springer, Heidelberg (2010)
24. Yun, H., Ha, D., Hwang, B., Ho Ryu, K.: Mining association rules on significant rare data using relative support. J. Syst. Softw. **67**(3), 181–191 (2003)

Recommendation Systems
and Ontologies

MA_THR: Multi-Agent Thai Herb Recommendation from Heterogeneous Data Sources

Ponrudee Netisopakul$^{(\boxtimes)}$ and Phakphoom Chainapaporn

Knowledge Management and Knowledge Engineering Laboratory,
Faculty of Information Technology, King Mongkut's Institute of Technology
Ladkrabang, Bangkok, Thailand
ponrudee@it.kmitl.ac.th, chphakphoom@gmail.com

Abstract. Multi-Agent Thai Herb Recommendation system (MA_THR) recommends Thai herb treatments based on a personal patient profile. Thai herb information is collected from available heterogeneous data sources, such as outside databases and websites. The collected information is integrated into a main Thai herb ontology, which is used as a knowledge base of the system. In order to integrate each component into one solution, multi-agent architecture is designed and implemented. The overall system evaluation justified by three human experts gives 89 % precision and 94 % recall.

Keywords: Multi-agent · Recommendation system · Thai herb

1 Introduction

Thai herbs have been used as a traditional medicine for a long time. History evidence shows that Thai herbs are used to treat many symptoms over 2,500 years ago [1]. Recently, Thai herb treatment increasingly gains attention. In USA, Thai herbs are accepted to use as an alternative drugs because Thai herb treatment causes few or no side effects. In Australia hospital, Thai herbs are offered to patients in order to treat many symptoms as an alternative or supplemental to modern medicine. The report by [2] states that Thai people has paid more than several ten billion baht per year for modern medicine, which treat only when symptoms appear; while Thai herb can also be used to promote holistic health.

The holistic system in Thai traditional culture is made up from four elements: Earth, Water, Air and Fire [3]. This element system is the basic of heath balancing. Traditional Thai treatment believes that an illness is caused by an unbalanced body element. To promote body element balance, Thai herbs with compatible tastes must be carefully chosen based on patient's body element. For example, a patient with earth element should consume Thai herb with acerbity, sweet, oily or salty taste.

Information on Thai herbs can be found on a number of websites, to name a few, Land of Thai Medicinal Plant [4], Herbal Medicine Lists and Uses [5], Thai herb database on the samunpri website [6]. They can be accessed either in a static form such as an html webpage or in a dynamic form by retrieving data from some backended databases. These websites provide similar information but details are varied.

A. Kawtrakul et al. (Eds.): ISIP 2013, CCIS 421, pp. 103–118, 2014.
DOI: 10.1007/978-3-319-08732-0_8, © Springer International Publishing Switzerland 2014

In order to integrate this valuable Thai herb information into one knowledge base and to use it to recommend Thai herb treatments to each patient personally, a multi-agent approach is proposed.

This paper is organized as follow. Section 2 describes the challenges and contributions of our research and briefly gives an overview of solutions. Section 3 reviews previous related research and point out how we have benefited and improved upon their work. Section 4 describes the process of multi-agent interactions to achieve two main objectives, those are, collecting Thai herb information from various sources and recommending the best Thai herb from the Thai herb knowledge base. Section 5 depicts our Thai herb knowledge base using ontology and describes the chaining of inference rules that are used to find suitable Thai herbs from each patient profile. The 6th section shows the experiment results related to each challenge and the human expert evaluation of the recommendation system.

2   The Challenges and Contributions

There are four challenging issues related to collecting, merging and recommending Thai herb treatment using data available from heterogeneous sources.

2.1   Challenging Issues

First challenge is that how to design a system to retrieve Thai herb information from various known sources, including one that allows an outside system to access its database, and one that only provides information on its website. In addition, the system should be able to easily plug-in another data source in the future, when one become available.

Second challenge is that how to extract pieces of desired information from a Thai text format; in particular, how to extract Thai herb part and it's medicinal-used from text. Figure 1(a) shows an excerpt input text from a webpage (the author provides English translation in parenthesis for readers). The text contains the part of Thai herb (a pod), and symptoms it can be used to treat, such as 'a laxative agent', 'emetine', 'parasite purging', 'malnutrition children', and 'malaria'. The desired output of extracted information is shown in Fig. 1(b). The proposed methodology used should be general enough to apply to most available text sources, at the same time; it should be efficient enough when working with itemized or well-defined webpages.

Third challenge, how to recognize and merge the same Thai herb from different sources. Each data source has its own style of presenting Thai herb information. Not only the formats of information are different, but also the contents of the information. For example, the two pieces of information in Fig. 2(a) and (b) are the same Thai herb but different details of information from two sources. The first webpage refers to a herb called "sadao-ban", which its stem can treat diarrhea and its fruit can be used to purge parasite and so on; while the second webpage refers to a herb called "sadao-tai", which its flower can treat blood poisoning and so on. Both of them are the same herb which can be recognized from their common other names. Hence, a desired

ฝัก ควรเก็บเมื่อแก่มีสีดำ นำมาตากให้แห้งเก็บไว้ใช้ ฝักมีกลิ่นเหมืน เอียน ๆ เฉพาะตัว ฝักที่ดีควรสมบูรณ์ ไม่มีก้าน เมื่อแห้งแล้วเขย่า

จะไม่มีเสียง ควรใช้ฝักประมาณ 30 กรัม ต้มกับน้ำกิน ในฝักจะมีสาร anthraquinone อยู่ ใช้ทำเป็นยาระบาย สำหรับผู้ที่ท้องผูก

เป็นประจำ หญิงมีครรภ์ใช้ฝักดูนเป็นยาระบายได้ นอกจากนี้ยังใช้ขับเสมหะ ขับพยาธิ รักษาเด็กที่เป็นโรคตานขโมย และ โรคไข้

มาลาเรียด้วย.....

(A pod should be reaped when it's old and black, and then dried for use later. The pod has its own special smell. The good pod should not have branches. When the dried pod is shaken, it should not produce a sound. When use, boil 30 Gram of the pod in water. The chemical compound called anthraquinone contained in the pod can be used as a <u>laxative</u> agent for alleviate a difficulty in defecation. Persons with constipation or pregnant women can use the pod as a <u>laxative</u>. In addition, it can be used as an <u>emetine</u> and <u>parasite purging</u>. The pod can also treat <u>malnutrition</u> children or children with <u>malaria</u>.....)

(a)

ฝัก (Pod)

- ยาระบาย (laxative)

- ขับเสมหะ (emetine)

- ขับพยาธิ (parasite purging)

- เด็กที่เป็นโรคตานขโมย (malnutrition)

- โรคไข้มาลาเรีย (malaria)

(b)

Fig. 1. (a) The input text of Thai herb's medicinal-used before extraction. (b) The desired itemized of Thai herb's part and its medicinal-used after extraction.

output is the merging of these two pieces of information into one as shown in Fig. 2(c).

Last challenge is how to recommend suitable Thai herb for a given patient in an expert system style. That is, the system should be able to give different recommendation based on each patient profile. The profile includes a patient's living places, a chronic disease, a birthdate, preferred and un-preferred tastes and so on. For example, supposed that there are two patients with diarrhea. One lives in the north region and other lives in the south region. The system should be able to recommend only a banana for the second patient and recommend both rosella and banana for the first patient based on the fact that banana grows everywhere in Thailand but rosella grows only in the north region.

Another example, if the patient would like to treat abdominal gas, which can be treated by many Thai herbs, such as ginger and leucaena. But this patient has cardiovascular diseases. The system should not recommend those Thai herbs which are prohibited from cardiovascular diseases, such as leucaena and should only recommend ginger.

2.2   Brief Description of Proposed Solution

In order to solve the above challenging issues in one unified system, we designed a multi-agent system consisting of multiple agents called Multi-Agent Thai Herb

Official name: สะเดาบ้าน (sadao-ban)

Other name: กะเดา สะเลียม (kadao, saluim)

Science name: Azadirachta indica A. Jass. var. siamensis Valeton

Family name: MELIACEAE

สรรพคุณ (treatment topic) เปลือกต้น แก้ท้องเดิน แก้บิดมูกเลือด ผล ยาถ่ายพยาธิ แก้ริดสีดวงทวาร แก้ปัสสาวะพิการ

(Stem can be used to treat diarrhea, dysentery. Fruit can be used to treat parasite purging, haemorrhoids and Anuria.)

(a)

Official name: สะเดาไทย (sadao-tai)

Other name: กะเดา สะเลียม (kadao, saluim)

Common name: Siamese neem tree, Nim , Margosa, Quinine

Science name: Azadirachta indica A. Juss. var. siamensis Valeton

Family name: Meliaceae

สรรพคุณ (treatment topic)

ดอก ยอดอ่อน - แก้พิษโลหิต กำเดา แก้ริดสีดวงในลำคอ...

(Flower can be used to treat blood poisoning, nosebleed, haemorrhoids in neck)

(b)

Official name: สะเดาบ้าน (sadao-ban) , สะเดาไทย (sadao-tai)

Other name: กะเดา สะเลียม (kadao, saluim)

Science name: Azadirachta indica A. Jass. var. siamensis Valeton

Family name: MELIACEAE

สรรพคุณ (treatment topic)

เปลือกต้น แก้ท้องเดิน แก้บิดมูกเลือด ผล ยาถ่ายพยาธิ แก้ริดสีดวงทวาร แก้ปัสสาวะพิการ

ดอก ยอดอ่อน - แก้พิษโลหิต กำเดา แก้ริดสีดวงในลำคอ...

(Stem can be used to treat diarrhea, dysentery. Fruit can be used to treat parasite purging, haemorrhoids and Anuria.

Flower can be used to treat blood poisoning, nosebleed, haemorrhoids in neck)

(c)

Fig. 2. Example of (a) Thai herb information on the first webpage. (b) Thai herb information on the second webpage. (c) The merging result of Thai herb information

Recommendation system (MA_THR). For Thai herb collection from heterogeneous data sources issue, two types of agents are designed to work with Thai herb information collection processes. One extracts information from database data sources; the other extracts information from webpage style data sources. Depending on the number of data sources, there can be more than one agent for each type of data source, one agent per one data source. In addition, the system may have to provide more than one non-homogenous agent to work with each type of data sources to handle different format and content of each data source. The detail of these will be elaborated in Sect. 4.

For the Thai herb content extraction issue, we use both html parser and template file containing key topics to extract wanted chunk of information from webpage's text. Then further process the chunk to obtain itemized information, such as Thai herb names, their part of used, a list of symptom names cured by the herb. These are handled by a number of Web Extraction Agents – WEA. The details of this process can be found at [7].

For the Thai herb integration issue, we design two algorithms, one for merging the same Thai herb information from two sources at a time, mainly using their names to decide whether they are the same Thai herb or not. Another algorithm is to integrate symptoms into one source, in order to consistently access them for recommendation. These are handled by a Source Merging Agent - SMA, with details can be found at [8].

The last issue and the focus of this paper, is the task of constructing an expert system called MA_THR, which stands for Multi-Agent Thai Herb Recommendation system. This can be achieved by incorporating Thai herb ontology and inference rules to recommend the most suitable Thai herb based on each patient profile.

Hence, there are four contributions associated with four challenging issues described above. A multi-agent architecture is proposed as an overall solution to solve a number of issues above and to integrate them into one system solution.

3   Related Works

There are number of related work, some proposed a multi-agent approach to search therapy result from remote medical system, such as a system called *Distributed Ay-urvedic Diagnosis and Therapy System for Hridroga using Agents (DADTSHUA)* [9]. Some focused on obtaining data from heterogeneous databases, such as [10]. Some are related to web content extraction aspects, such as [11, 12]. Some concentrated on solving word similarity such as [13–15]. Finally, there are works that recommend Thai herb based on a patient profile, such as [16, 17]. Our work has benefits greatly from these previous works but none of them above have done what we have done in our work. The summarization of previous research with related problem, their advantage and disadvantage, and most importantly, how we adopt and adapt the ideas to our work is explained in Table 1.

4   The Overall System

The MA_THR system is powered by a multi-agent architecture. The system can be divided into two subsystems as shown in Fig. 3. The first subsystem is front-end; this subsystem is responsible for recommending Thai herbs based on a patient's symptom and profile. The second subsystem is back-end, which is responsible for collecting Thai herb from heterogeneous data sources. The details of each subsystem are described as follows.

4.1   Front-End Subsystem

The main function of this module is to recommend Thai herb for treating a patient's symptom. There are two components: a user interface agent and a recommendation module with a number of collaborative agents. An input output agent - IOA is the

Table 1. Summarize of related work

Previous research: Related problem	Advantages and disadvantages	Improvement
A model of distributed ayurvedic diagnosis and therapy system for Hridroga [9] : Multi-agent architecture design and application	A: The design enables same types of agents to collaborate seamlessly. D: Every host must have the same set of agents; hence, it cannot support heterogeneous data processing	We redesign our system based-on three tier layer in order to easily plug-in Thai herb data sources in the future
Heterogeneous database integration of ERP system based on OGSA-DAI [10] : Heterogeneous database integration	A: Database schema mapping table is used to access remote database from a one stop service center. D: The process is not automated; it must be prepared and initialized by a human user	We apply the idea of source schema mapping toward both database and website integration with improvement on automation
Design and implementation of a web news extraction system [11] : Information extraction from multiple websites	A: HTML parser and regular expression to extract the main text content on websites. D: It cannot used to extract text contain various embedded detail such as the one in each Thai herb webpages	We apply HTML parser and regular expression to extract Thai herb names but we also develop our information extraction process to extract other details
Ontology directed semantic annotation process [12] : Information extraction from multiple websites	A: Needed information is extracted from websites using ontology D: Vocabulary list must be manually prepared in the ontology	We do not use ontology during information extraction process We only use ontology as a knowledge base during recommendation process
Surname spellings and computerized record linkage [13], binary codes capable of correcting deletions, insertions, and reversals [14] : Similar name matching	A: They proposed an algorithm to calculate similarity of names base-on character-matched and character-unmatched D: The algorithm cannot apply to synonyms with different set of alphabets	We develop an exact name matching algorithm to identify the same Thai herb from different sources
Verb semantics and lexical selection [15] : Finding synonyms	A: It proposed to use wordnet to find synonyms D: Some languages have no wordnet resource	We develop a domain dependent knowledge to calculate similarities of symptoms
An E-Health advice system with Thai herb and an ontology [17], Ontology-based E-Health system with Thai herb recommendation [16]	A: A recommendation system that uses a patient profile to recommend Thai herb D: It is not clear how many data sources are used. In addition, the work did not consider a patient element and both did not recommend the best Thai herb	We have similar ontology but used various Thai herb data sources to give more extensive recommendation and have inference rules to find a best Thai herb for each patient based on the profile and body element

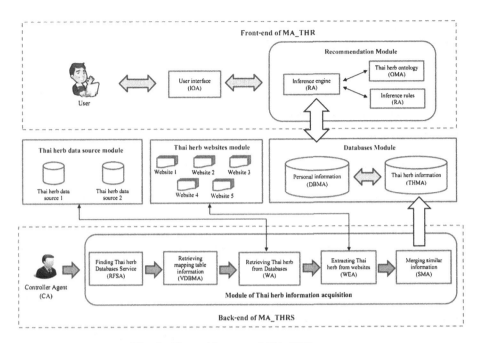

Fig. 3. The architecture of MA_THR system

agent that is responsible for the user interface. It receives patient symptom and sends it to the recommendation module, it also receives the recommendation result back and display it to the user. The recommendation module is driven by recommendation agents - RA and an ontology management agent - OMA. In order to successfully recommend Thai herb, it must consult with Thai herb ontology and a set of inference rules. The process of Thai herb recommendation can be divided into 3 steps

- The first step, RA connects to Thai herb Ontology Management Agent (OMA) for loading Thai herb ontology.
- The second step, RA connects to DBMA to retrieve Thai herb information that is previously collected and stored in the databases. It then creates instances of Thai herbs in the loaded Thai herb ontology.
- The last step, RA load inference rules and start a forward inference chain to obtain the best the Thai herb that can treat patient's symptom.

The details of Thai herb ontology design and inference rules are described in the Sect. 5.

4.2 Back-End Subsystem

As we mention earlier, the back-end subsystem is responsible for collecting Thai herb information from various databases and multiple websites. In addition, it is also responsible for identifying the same Thai herb from different sources and merging their information into one. The back-end processes are initiated and automated by a center agent - CA. There are five main processes.

Finding Thai Herb Databases Services

In order to access Thai herb information from different Thai herb databases services, CA must connect to another agent called register and finding service agent – RFSA, to obtain available addresses of each Thai herb databases service.

Retrieving Information Map Table

In order to map database field names to Thai herb information in a form of xml schema, a database schema mapping table similar to the one proposed by [10] is used. An agent called virtual database mapping agent - VDBMA is responsible for managing this mapping table. Figure 4 shows an excerpt from the mapping table.

The tag *<thaiHerbKnowledgeBase>* contains a virtual table schema, while the tag *<dataSource address="thaiHerbKnowledgeService1">* refers to an address name of Thai herb database service and its mapping to the virtual table. The sub tag *<table-Name>* maps the virtual table name to the source database table name, while the sub tags *<fieldNames>* maps the virtual table field names to the source database table field name.

Thai Herb Information Extraction from Multiple Websites

Thai herb information can also be found on many websites. In order to extract needed information correctly, we have to develop and implement algorithms into the web extraction agent – WEA.

First, WEA need to identify 'chunk' of information on particular webpage containing Thai herb information. This chunk has certain *topics* we want to extract, such

```
<thaiHerbKnowledgeService>
    <normalTable name="nameOfThaiHerb">
        <normalField> thaiName </normalField>
        <normalField> scienceName </normalField>
        ...........................
    </normalTable>
    <thaiHerbService adress="thaiHerbKnowledgeService1">
        <tableService refer="nameOfThaiHerb">
            <sourceFieldMap>
                <field normalField ="thaiName"> NAMETHAIHERB.NAMETHAIOFFICE </field>
                <field normalField ="scienceName"> NAMETHAIHERB.SCIENCENAME </field>
                ....................
            </sourceFieldMap>
            <sourceTable>
                <table> NAMETHAIHERB </table>
            </sourceTable>
        </tableService>
    </thaiHerbService>
</thaiHerbKnowledgeService>
```

Fig. 4. Thai herb information mapping table.

as names (science name, family name, common name, etc.), parts of used and symptom names. While JSOUP and HTML parser can be employed to successfully extract chunks from some well-defined structure webpages, a more complicated method involving *relevant topic identification and chunk extraction* must be invented to extract chunks from more complicated or inconsistent structure webpages.

Second, this extracted chunk needs to be further processed to extract *content* for each specific topic. One Thai herb can have many parts of used and can cure many symptoms. While regular expressions can be used to separate parts-of-used, the most difficult information to extract are symptom names associated with a Thai herb or a part-of-used, as shown in Fig. 1(b). We employed an iterative learning process to *learn* symptom names. First, a list of symptom names is extracted using their proximity to *treating words (cure, treat, etc.)* and their synonyms. Then the list is scanned against other chunks from various webpages. Using this approach, [7] reported the combined results of 4 websites has improved symptom names extraction accuracies from 72 % to 86 % in f-measure. More details of this process have been explained in our previous work [7].

Merging Similar Thai Herb Information

The main problem of collecting information from heterogeneous data sources is how to integrating those information into one usable source. That is how to identify the same Thai herb from different sources, which may be called by different names, and how to identify the same symptom that called by different names, and finally, how to merge them into one source without losing the original information. An agent called sourcing and merging agent - SMA is responsible for these tasks.

Note that for the nature of this domain, there is no *contradictory* case, i.e., a webpage A says an herb H1 can treat a symptom S1, but a webpage B says it cannot. Only *complimentary* cases exist, i.e., a website A says that a herb H1 can treat symptoms S1 and S2 and a website B says that a herb H1 (which may be called by another name) can treat symptoms S3 and S4. Hence, two tasks involve in this step are to identify the same Thai herb with different names from different sources and to find the same symptom with different names. The details of both parts are described in [8]. The results of this component are sent to Thai herb information management agent – THMA, to store them in Thai herb information database.

4.3   Multi-agent Interaction

In order to work successfully, each agent must communication to each other. The communication protocol of multi-agent in MA_THR follows the guideline in [18]. It consists of two processes: (1) Thai herb collection from heterogeneous data sources process and (2) Thai herb recommendation process.

Thai Herb Collection from Heterogeneous Data Sources

This process collects Thai herbs from various websites and databases For the purpose of updating information, the process can be set to start working periodically, for example, automatically collect data every 7 days. A center agent - CA is responsible for initiated and automated this process. Other agents involving in this process are wrapper agent – WA, responsible for source database connection; register and finding service agent – RFSA, responsible for obtaining an IP address and platform of WA; virtual database management agent – VDBMA, responsible for mapping data schema to a virtual knowledge base schema; sourcing and merging agent – SMA, responsible for integrating Thai herb information retrieved from various sources; and finally, Thai herb management agent – THMA, responsible for storing the integrated Thai herb information into Thai herb XML file. The flow of the process is shown in Fig. 5(a).

Thai Herb Recommendation Process

This process searches for suitable Thai herbs base on each patient's profile. Through GUI of the input output service – IOA, a patient enters a symptom that need to be treated. Then, the IOA sends a *RequestCAAdress* message to the RFSA to obtain the IP address and platform of CA. After obtaining the address, the IOA then sends a *RequestRecommend* message to the CA with the content of the message containing the symptom name and the username. The CA sends a *RequestPersonalInformation* message to the DBMA to retrieve the patient's profile, such as birthday, chronic disease, preferred taste, un-preferred taste and so on.

Now the CA forwards the responding patient's information to the recommendation agent - RA using a *RequestInferenceThaiHerb* message. The RA forwards a *RequestThaiHerbInformation* message to the THMA to retrieve Thai herb information from the Thai herb XML file. After obtaining Thai herb information, the RA connects to ontology management agent - OMA using a *RequestOntology* message.

The RA, with the help of OMA, uses Thai herb information and the patient's information to instantiate instances in the Thai herb ontology. Finally, the RA uses the inference rules to find the best Thai herb for the patient. The RA sends Thai herb recommendation back to the CA using a *GetResultInferrenceThaiHerb* message.

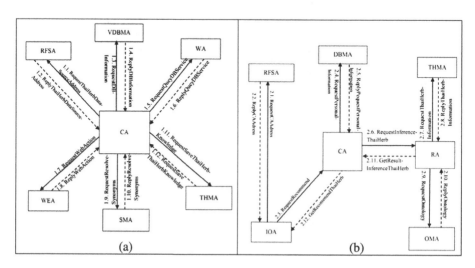

Fig. 5. The process of (a) Thai herb collection from heterogeneous data sources using multi-agent and (b) Thai herb treatment recommendation using multi-agent

Then, the CA forwards the Thai herb recommendation using a *GetRecommendThai-Herb* message back to the IOA, in order to display the result to the patient. The process flow is shown in Fig. 5(b).

5   Thai Herb Ontology and Inference Rules

5.1   Thai Herb Ontology Design

We adapted our Thai herb ontology from the ontology in [16] and extended it using some concepts from Thai herb books [19, 20]. There are seven main classes with totally 39 main and sub-classes, 28 object properties and 18 datatype properties.

Figure 6 illustrates the eight main classes in our ontology, namely ThaiHerb, PartOfUse, Symptom, Person, Element, Location, Taste and ChronicDieases. The six classes here are identical to the classes in the work by [16], except the PartOfUse and the Element class.

The element class is our supplement base on Thai traditional treatment. However, there is no need for a patient to enter the element information because the system can map a patient's month of birth to his/her body element using information in Table 2. This information also leads to the taste(s) of Thai herb matched to the patient.

5.2   Inference Rules

Our system used JESS as an inference engine. The rules can be divided into 2 sets. The first rule set, with 12 rules, is used to find the patient's element. Another rule set is used to find the best Thai herbs base on patient's profile. We have designed the forward inference chaining, supplementing with point accumulation when matched

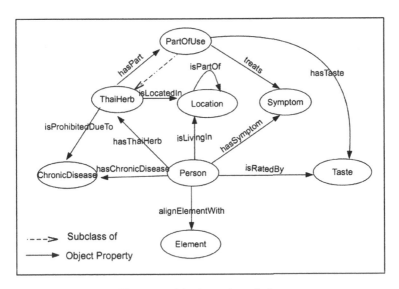

Fig. 6. Thai herb ontology design

Table 2. The month of birth and compatible taste(s) for each element

Elements	Month of birth	Tasted
Earth	October, November, December	Acerbity, sweet, oily, salty
Water	July, August, September	Bitter, acidulous
Air	April, May, June	Spicy
Fire	January, February, March	Bitter, tasteless

Thai herb is found. Thai herbs that get the highest point from these rules are recommended to the patient. An output example is shown in Fig. 7.

In order to easily understand the process of Thai herb recommendation, suppose a patient is Phakphoom Chainapaporn, whose birthmonth is in November, as shown in Fig. 7, he lives in Phuket, he has diarrhea and his chronic disease is cardiopathy, his preferred taste is sweet and not preferred taste is acerbity.

The first rule for classifying patient's body element *rule_findElementForNov* is activated. The Earth element is added into the patient's profile. Afterwards, the second rule *rule_goodThaiherbForTheSymptom* is activated to find a set of candidate Thai herbs which can treat the diarrhea. There are five Thai herbs found: *banana, pomegranate, guava, anacardium occidentale* and *cork wood tree.*

The third activation involving a number of rules; those are *rule_goodThaiHerb_ForElemenEarth, rule_goodThaiHerb_ForLivingPlace, rule_goodThaiHerb_WithNotPerferredTaste, rule_goodThaiHerb_ButProhibitedChronicDisease* and *rule_goodThaiHerb_WithPerferredTaste.* If any positive result is found, a plus point is added, if any negative result is found, a minus point is added. The output of those rules can be explained as follow. All five Thai herbs from the second activation are suitable for *the patient's element* and can be found in the *patient's living place.* Thai herbs those are *not* compatible to *patient's taste* are *Pomegranate* and *Guava.*

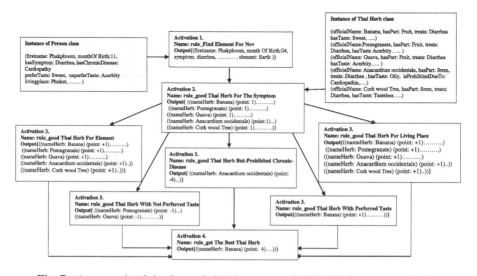

Fig. 7. An example of the forward chaining process for Thai herb recommendation

The *anacardium occidentale* is *prohibited* by *patient's chronic disease*. *Banana* is good for all conditions. Finally, the final rule activation is *rule_getTheBestThaiHerb*, which recommend *Banana* with the highest point score of 4.

6   Experiments

There are mainly 4 experiments. The first experiment is to validate the usefulness of a multi-agent architecture system versus a traditional component-based system. We found that when the number of data sources increases, execution times of both architectures grow exponentially. However, an execution time of a multi-agent architecture grows much slower than the traditional one, as shown in Fig. 8.

The second experiment is setup to preliminary evaluate an efficiency of the extraction algorithm. A hundred webpages from five available Thai herb information websites are randomly selected; hence there are totally a hundred Thai herbs. The extraction can identify all Thai herbs. It can also identify most of the details of Thai herbs correctly, as shown in Table 3. The result for various types of name extraction ranges from 98 to 100 % in f-measure, for part-of-used extraction is 93 % and for symptom name extraction is 87 % in f-measure, respectively.

After the second experiment, the system is fully run. It then collects totally 1367 Thai herbs from different sources, including from available Thai herb databases. The third experiment integrates these Thai herbs into one database using extended name matching algorithm. In addition, synonym symptom names must be identified and integrated. The merging results of synonym Thai herbs and synonym symptoms are shown in Table 4, with accuracies of 93 % and 97.6 %, respectively.

Finally, the fourth experiment is to evaluate correctness of MA_THR recommendation system by randomizing 100 patient profiles as input for Thai herb recommendation. The precision and recall are calculated based on 3 human expert

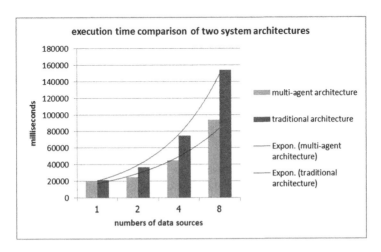

Fig. 8. Execution time comparison of multi-agent vs. traditional architecture

Table 3. Result of extracting Thai herbs from 100 webpages

	Correct	Incorrect	Available	Precision	Recall	f-measure
Formal name	100	0	100	100	100	100
Science name	103	0	105	100	98	99
Common name	101	0	102	100	99	100
Local name	487	5	500	99	97	98
Family name	100	1	101	99	99	99
Part of used	208	12	225	95	92	93
Symptom	667	78	789	90	85	87

Table 4. Results of Thai herb integration (left): Thai herb merging (right): symptom merging

Synonym Thai herbs merging	# of synonym Thai herbs	# of not synonyms Thai herbs	Total	Synonym symptoms merging	# of synonym symptom	# of not synonym symptoms	Total
Merged	274	29	303	Similarity greater than or equals 0.6	716	78	794
Not merged	15	319	334	Similarity less than 0.6	1656	68966	70622
Total	289	348	637	Total	2372	69044	71416
Accuracy	(274 + 319)* 100/637		93 %	Accuracy	(716 + 68966)* 100/71416		97.6 %

opinions. For precision, we count a number of recommended Thai herbs that are agreed with at least 1, 2 and 3 expert opinions. For recall, we also count a number of additional recommended Thai herbs that is suggested by any expert.

The number of all Thai herbs recommended by the system is 398. There are 354, 319, and 281 Thai herbs that are agreed with at least 1, 2 and 3 expert opinions, respectively. There are 24 Thai herbs that are additionally suggested by experts. Therefore, the efficiency of Thai herb recommendation based on at least 1, 2 and 3 expert agreements are 89 %, 81 % and 71 % in precisions and 94 %, 93 % and 92 % in recalls.

7   Conclusion

This paper presents the architecture and the process of Thai herb collection and recommendation from heterogeneous data sources by using multi-agent and ontology. Specifically, the multi-agent architecture is proposed to unify various components into one system. The information collected will be stored to our own designed Thai herb ontology. The benefit of using ontology is to seamlessly integrate with inference engine in our Thai herb recommendation system. For the process of Thai herb recommendation, this paper has presented the design of Thai herb ontology and inference rules in order to recommend Thai herbs that are suitable for each patient profile. MA_THR is not only recommend Thai herb that is used to treat the patient's symptom but also find the best Thai herb matches to each patient conditions including the body element. In our experiment, we measure the precision and recall of Thai herb recommendation by three human experts and obtain as high as 89 % precision and 94 % recall.

References

1. Salguero, C.: A Thai Herbal. Findhorn Press, Scotland (2003)
2. Chokevivat, V., Chuthaputti, A.: The role of Thai traditional medicine in health promotion. In: The 6th Global Conference on Health Promotion, Bangkok, pp. 1–25 (2005)
3. Chawapradit, P.: The body element knowledge for take care the health and mind. In: Bureau of agricultural Commodities Promotion and Management (2013) http://www.agriman.doae.go.th/home/news3/news3_1/samunpri/0047_Note(20.03.12).pdf. Accessed October 2013
4. Mahidol University: Land of Thai medicinal plant. In: Siri Ruckhachati Nature Park (2010). http://www.pharmacy.mahidol.ac.th/siri. Accessed 17 May 2010
5. Plant Genetic Conservation Project Office: Herbal medicine lists and uses. In: Herbal Medicine Lists and Uses. http://rspg.or.th/plants_data/herbs/herbs_200.htm
6. samunpridotcom: Thai herb database. In: samunpridotcom. http://www.samunpri.com
7. Chainapaporn, P., Netisopakul, P.: Thai herb information extraction from multiple websites. In: 2012 4th International Conference on Knowledge and Smart Technology (KST), Chonburi, pp. 16–23 (2012)
8. Chainapaporn, P., Netisopakul, P.: Word similarity algorithm for merging Thai herb information from heterogeneous data sources. In: Proceedings of 5th International Conference on Information Technology and Electrical Engineering, Jogyakarta, pp. 159–163 (2013)
9. Raj, E.S., Idicula, S.M.: A model of distributed ayurvedic diagnosis and therapy system for hridroga using agents. In: World Congress on Nature & Biologically Inspired Computing 2009, pp. 1378–1381 (2009)
10. Liu, X., Shi, Y., Xu, Y., Tian, Y., Liu, F.: Heterogeneous database integration of EPR system based on OGSA-DAI. In: Zhang, W., Chen, Z., Douglas, C.C., Tong, W. (eds.) HPCA 2009. LNCS, vol. 5938, pp. 257–263. Springer, Heidelberg (2010)
11. Xia, H.-L., Zhang, Y.-S.: Design and implementation of a web news extraction system. In: 2011 Eighth International Conference on Fuzzy Systems and Knowledge Discovery (FSKD), Shanghai, pp. 1793–1797 (2011)
12. Kuptabut, S., Netisopakul, P.: Ontology directed semantic annotation process. In: 3rd International Conference on Information Sciences and Interaction Sciences, Chengdu, pp. 251–255 (2010)
13. Guth, G.: Surname spellings and computerized record linkage. Hist. Meth. Newsl. 10(1), 10–19 (1976)
14. Levenshtein, V.: Binary codes capable of correcting deletions, insertions, and reversals. Sov. Phys. Dokl. 10, 10–19 (1966)
15. Wu, Z., Palmer, M.: Verb semantics and lexical selection. In: Proceedings of the 32nd Annual Meeting of the Association for Computational Linguistics, New Mexico, pp. 133–138 (1994)

16. Kato, T., Maneerat, N., Varakulsiripunth, R., Kato, Y., Takahashi, K.: Ontology-based E-health system with Thai herb recommendation. In: The 6th International Joint Conference on Computer Science and Software, Phuket, pp. 172–177 (2009)

17. Nantiruj, T., Maneerat, N., Varakulsiripunth, R., Izumi, S., Shiratori, N., Kato, T., Kato, Y., Takahashi, K.: An E-Health advice system with Thai herb and an ontology. In: The 3rd International Symposium on Biomedical Engineering, Bangkok, pp. 315–319 (2008)

18. Bellifemine, F., Carie, G., Greenwood, D.: Developing Multi-Agent System with JADE. Wiley, Chichester (2007)

19. Chotanan: Thai Herb for Public Health. Duangkamon, Bangkok (2008)

20. Matchachip, S.: Thai Herb. Phrae-Phitthaya, Bangkok (2000)

21. Chainapaporn, P., Netisopakul, P.: Multi-agent architecture for Thai herb recommendation. In: 9th Joint International Symposium on Natural Language Processing and Agricultural Ontology Service, Bangkok, pp. 1–6 (2011)

22. Dasgupta, S., Papadimitriou, C., Vazirani, U.: Algorithms. McGraw-Hill, New York (2006)

Ontology Design Approaches for Development of an Excise Duty Recommender System

Marut Buranarach[1]([⊠]), Taneth Ruangrajitpakorn[1],
Chutiporn Anutariya[2], and Vilas Wuwongse[3]

[1] Language and Semantic Technology Laboratory,
National Electronics and Computer Technology Center (NECTEC),
Klong Luang, Pathumthani, Thailand
{marut.bur,taneth.rua}@nectec.or.th
[2] School of Information Technology, Shinawatra University,
Samkhok, Pathumthani, Thailand
chutiporn@siu.ac.th
[3] Faculty of Engineering, Thammasat University, Klong Luang,
Pathumthani, Thailand
wvilas@engr.tu.ac.th

Abstract. Excise duty is a type of tax charged on certain products and services. Determining an excise product class can be a difficult task since the regulation written in legal language can be difficult for the users to interpret. Excise duty recommender system aims to simplify the users' effort in product classification task and reduce errors in tax payment. This paper describes an initiative to develop excise product ontology to provide explicit and formal definitions of excise products and their classifications. It focuses on ontology design approaches for some excise products to support excise duty recommender system development. Two excise products were used as case studies: beverage and petroleum products. Steps in defining product mapping rules and developing the recommender system are described. A Semantic Web-based system architecture was adopted to enable future support for data sharing and reuse based on the Linked Data technology.

Keywords: Excise product ontology · Tax recommender system · Semantic Web-based information system

1 Introduction

Excise duty is a type of tax charged on certain products and services. It usually targets at products and services that are considered unnecessary or luxurious. Unlike general sales tax, excise tax may be charged proportional to the retail price of the products or per product unit. Some common products that excise duty are applied to include petroleum, beverage, automobile, liquor, and tobacco products, etc. Classification of excise product is necessary to determine the rate of excise duty on a product.

Regulation of the products and their tax rates are usually based on certain characteristics of the products. However, determining a class for some excise products can be a difficult task. This is generally due to the lack of unambiguous and formal definition of excise products. Description of product class based on the regulation is

A. Kawtrakul et al. (Eds.): ISIP 2013, CCIS 421, pp. 119–127, 2014.
DOI: 10.1007/978-3-319-08732-0_9, © Springer International Publishing Switzerland 2014

generally written in legal language, which is difficult to interpret by the users. Excise duty recommender system that can assist in excise product classification can greatly simplify the users' effort and reduce errors in tax payment.

In our project, we aimed to develop excise ontology for the Thailand Excise Department. Some benefits of developing excise ontology include providing explicit and formal definitions of excise products and their classifications. The ontology can help in reducing ambiguity and inconsistency in determining an excise duty class for a product. In addition, excise ontology can be shared and reused within and across organizations. This paper discusses some design approaches for excise ontology development. Two excise products are used as case studies: beverage and petroleum products. The scope of the ontology was primarily for supporting excise duty recommender system development. Implementation details of defining product mapping rules and architecture for the recommender system are described.

The paper is organized as follows. Section 2 describes motivations and methodology for excise product ontology development. Section 3 focuses on some unique design approaches for excise product ontology using two case study products. Section 4 presents design and implementation of an ontology-based excise duty recommender system. Section 5 provides conclusion and some future development directions.

2 Ontology for Excise Products

2.1 Roles of Excise Ontology

Roles and benefits of ontology in AI and Law are generally recognized [1–4]. Ontology helps in organizing and structuring legal information and searching [4]. Ontology can support domain knowledge sharing and reuse [4]. In addition, mapping of legal knowledge from natural language to some formal syntax and semantics can enable automated reasoning [3]. Legal ontologies generally contain a mix of legal concepts and real-world concepts [3]. Thus, legal ontology may be classified based on whether it contains which of the two types of concepts. Tax ontology is a form of legal ontology that focuses on modeling tax-related knowledge to support intelligent applications such as automatic auditing, online help and tax question-answering systems [5]. These applications can help the users in reducing cost of tax advisors, reducing time and effort, and reducing errors [5].

Our initiative aims to develop excise ontology for the Thailand Excise Department. Some benefits of developing excise ontology include providing explicit and formal descriptions of excise products and their classifications. The ontology can help in reducing ambiguity and inconsistency in determining an excise duty class for a product. In addition, excise ontology can be shared and reused within and across organizations. Some potential applications of the excise ontology are discussed as follows:

(a) **Form consolidation.** By defining standard structure of excise product, it can reduce inconsistency in form fields design. Different form templates can be generated based on the structure defined in the excise product ontology. Form consolidation helps to prevent inconsistency in user's input data caused by inconsistent form fields.

(b) **Reference documentation.** By providing explicit definition of excise product classes and properties, human-readable version of the ontology can be generated as reference documentation for the user. In addition, labels and annotations defined in different languages can provide the source for creating multi-lingual documentation.

(c) **Excise Duty Recommender System.** Excise product ontology can be used in defining product-class mapping rules for automatic classification of excise products. In supporting excise duty recommender system, the ontology can be used as the schema for the knowledge base and to support reasoning about user products based on the defined mapping rules.

2.2   Excise Ontology Development Process

The excise ontology development process started from identification and acquisition of the related knowledge. Three knowledge sources were identified: paper-based forms, legal documents and domain experts. Paper-based forms contain various form fields related to excise products. These forms and form fields were thoroughly analyzed to generalize about classes and properties that are related to excise products. This "bottom-up" analysis approach allowed some general concepts to be identified and further refined in the next steps.

Another knowledge source was legal documents, i.e. law and regulations on excise products. Key concepts related to each product were identified based on the regulations on the product classification. This "top-down" analysis approach allowed some product-specific concepts, which are related to product classification, to be additionally identified. Domain experts were also consulted for resolving ambiguities and inconsistencies found in the reference documents. The analysis results were verified by the domain experts.

The next steps involved organization and refinement of the collected knowledge. Specifically, classes and properties and their relations for excise products were defined and represented in ontology. The scope of the ontology was mainly restricted to product characteristics and product classes. Two types of ontology were created: non-product-specific and product-specific ontology. The non-product-specific ontology contains the classes and properties used by all excise products. The product-specific ontology extends the non-product-specific one and contains the classes and properties used only by each product. By adopting the modular ontology design approach, it can facilitate ontology maintenance and extension. In the final step, public hearing sessions were conducted with the experts for verification and approval of the ontology for each product.

3   Ontology Design Approaches

This section discusses issues and challenges in designing excise product ontology. The discussion focuses on identifying classes and properties related to excise products. Two products are used to illustrate the design approaches: beverage and petroleum products. Both products were chosen because they share similar approaches in ontology design, although the petroleum product ontology is more complex, in terms of number of classes and properties. The approaches in defining classes and properties in the ontology are discussed as follows.

3.1 Product Classes

Two main classes are identified: product class and excise product class. Product class represents real-world view of products that is independent of excise view of products. Excise product class is based on excise product classification scheme, which is defined by laws. Specifically, it is a classification of excise products based on tax rates. For example, a beverage product may be considered a member of "energy drink" product class and considered a member of "flavored non-alcoholic beverage, not including fruit or vegetable juices" excise product class. Product class and excise product class each constitute its own class hierarchy. Product class contains product properties related to product characteristics. Excise product class contains product properties related to applied tax.

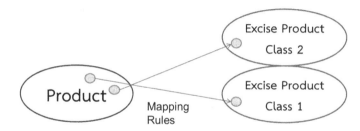

Fig. 1. Relationship between sets of products and excise product classes

An instance of a product class will be inferred as an instance of an excise product class based on some defined mapping rules. Specifically, a product whose class and property values are matched with the mapping rules will be concluded to be a member of an excise product class. Relationship between sets of product and excise product classes is illustrated in Fig. 1. Excise product classes are typically mutually exclusive, i.e., no product belongs to two classes, and all-inclusive, i.e., every product belongs to a class. Such a design approach will result in unambiguous product mapping results.

3.2 Product Properties

Product properties for both products were defined in four dimensions: physical, compound, usage or purpose, and identification dimensions. Properties in physical dimension included those related to external appearance of the product, such as volume, packaging, color, etc. These properties may be used to determine excise product class. For example, a beverage product sold in a higher-volume container must pay higher tax rate. Petroleum product usually put different color marker to identify its product type and thus can be used to determine excise product class and tax rate. Properties in the compound dimension include those related to ingredients or elements of the product. For beverage product, the properties in this dimension include ingredients and their proportions such as sweetener, flavored, carbonated, stimulant, caffeine, fruit-or-vegetable juice, etc. For petroleum product, they include chemical components and their proportions such as Ethanol, Lead, Methyl Ester of Fatty Acid, Sulfur, pureness, etc. Properties for specifying usage or purpose of product are also important in determining excise product class. For example, petroleum or beverage products that are produced and sold for charity or export purposes belong to different classes of tax rates. Properties in identification dimension include product name, and brand, etc. These properties are typically not used in the product mapping rules. Figure 2 shows dimensions of product properties for beverage and petroleum products.

A product property may be a shared property or product-specific property. Shared properties are typically common properties shared by all products. For excise product, shared properties are mostly properties in the identification dimension such as product name and brand. Product-specific properties are those unique to each product. Thus they cannot be shared between different products. The product-specific properties are mostly those in physical, compound and usage or purpose dimensions. These properties are typically used in the product mapping rules. Figure 3 shows portions of the beverage and petroleum product ontologies created using Protégé ontology editor. The beverage product ontology contains 28 classes and 28 object and data properties. The petroleum product ontology contains 90 classes and 46 object and data properties.

	Beverage Products	Petroleum Products
Physical	Package type, Volume	Color
Compound	Sweetener, Flavored, Carbonated, Fruit-or-Vegetable ingredients, Stimulant, Caffeine	Ethanol, Lead, Methyl Ester of Fatty Acid, Sulfur, Pureness
Usage/ Purpose	Drink making machine, Exported product, Donation	Purpose of sale, Place of sale, Buyer, Exported product
Identification	Product name, Brand	Product name, Brand

Fig. 2. Product property dimensions for beverage and petroleum products

4 Excise Duty Recommender System

Excise duty recommender system can alleviate the user' effort in determining excise product class for a product. Customers and officers can use the system to support decision making and verification. The excise product ontology is used as the standard schema for each excise product that can be used with the product mapping rules. The system is built on top of the Ontology Application Management (OAM) framework [6]. Implementation details of the excise duty recommender system and product mapping rules are provided as follows.

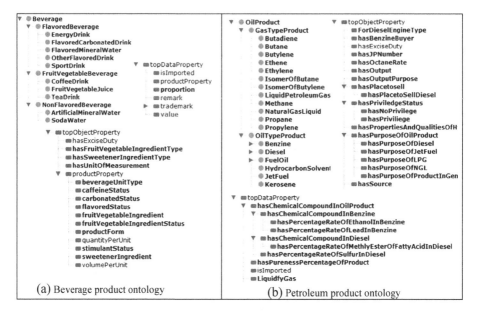

Fig. 3. Portions of the beverage and petroleum product ontology

4.1 Product Mapping Rules

Product mapping rules specify conditions of product properties and their concluded excise product classes. The steps in defining mapping rules for an excise product are described as follows. For each product, listing of all relevant product properties were created along with all possible values or range of values for each property. Each rule defines a possible combination of the property values and its concluded excise product class. The next step was to eliminate redundant rules. Specifically, rules that conclude the same excise product class for every possible value of a property were merged into one rule. Figure 4 shows an example of creating product mapping rules and eliminating redundant rules.

	Product Type	Product Property 1		...	Product Property n		Excise Product Class
		Value/ Range 1	Value/ Range 2		Value/ Range 1	Value/ Range 2	
Rule 1	A	X				X	B
Rule 2	A		X			X	B
Rule 12	A					X	B

Fig. 4. An example of creating product mapping rules and eliminating redundant rules

The defined mapping rules were inputted into the system using a recommendation editor provided by the OAM framework that hides complexity of rule language syntax. The OAM framework automatically transformed the created rules into rule language syntax used by a rule-based inference engine, i.e., Jena rule-based inference engine [7]. The generated rules were subsequently processed by the inference engine for producing the recommendation results. Figure 5 shows an example mapping rule for the beverage product created using the OAM framework.

```
[Tax_class_recommendation_instance_id_1: (?x1 rdf:type ns:tax_class_02_01) ->
(ns:tax_class_recommendation_instance_id_1 ns:has_rec_tax_class ?x1)
(ns:tax_class_recommendation_instance_id_1 ns:has_rec_result 'Tax class 02.01')
(ns:tax_class_recommendation_instance_id_1 rdf:type ns:tax_class_recommendation)]


[Linking_tax_class_recommendation_instance_id_1_to_beverage_product_0: (?x
rdf:type ns:beverage_product) (?x ns:has_flavored_status ?y0) (?y0 rdf:type
ns:non_flavored) (?x ns:has_fruit_vegetable_ingredient_status ?y1) (?y1 rdf:type
ns:no_fruit_vegetable_ingredient) -> (?x ns:has_suggested_tax_class
ns:tax_class_recommendation_instance_id_1)]
```

Fig. 5. An example mapping rule for the beverage product created using the OAM framework

4.2 System Architecture

The excise duty recommender system was developed using a Semantic Web-based system architecture. This is to enable future support for data sharing and reused based on the RDF data standard, i.e., Linked data. The system was implemented using the Ontology Application Management (OAM) framework. OAM framework is an application development platform that simplifies creation and adoption of ontology-based semantic web application [6]. Information about the user' products can be obtained from an excise product database. The framework facilitated mapping between the excise product database and the excise product ontology. The framework

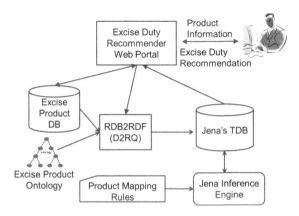

Fig. 6. System architecture of the excise duty recommender system

adopted the D2RQ system [8] in creating RDF data from relational database. The RDF data were stored in the Jena's TDB triple store and were processed by Jena inference engine based on the product mapping rules. The recommendation results were stored in the triple store and can be retrieved using the OAM API. The excise duty recommender web portal manages the interactions between the user, the database and the framework to produce recommendation results based on the product information. Figure 6 shows the system architecture of the excise duty recommender system.

5   Conclusion

This paper describes ontology design approaches for excise products focusing on supporting excise duty recommender system development. Some advantages of excise product ontology include providing standard structure and semantics for the excise product domain and allowing knowledge sharing and reuse within and across systems. The ontology design approaches were exemplified using the beverage and petroleum products. Product mapping rules were defined based on the product ontology to support excise product classification. An excise duty recommender system was developed using a Semantic Web-based system architecture to permit future data sharing and reuse. Excise product database, which contains the user-provided product information and laboratory verification results, may be used as input data to the system.

Some future work includes evaluation of the recommendation result accuracy. In addition, ontology will be developed for various types of excise products and services. Description Logic (DL) implementation of product mapping rules which would allow the mapping rules to be embedded within the ontology will be investigated. Our project also plans to adopt the Linked Data approach to integrating the excise product data with the related data, such as the Harmonized System tariff classification[1].

Acknowledgment. This work is supported by the Excise Department, Thailand.

References

1. Valente, A.: Legal Knowledge Engineering: A Modelling Approach. IOS Press, Amsterdam (1995)
2. Casellas, N.: Legal ontologies. In: Legal Ontology Engineering, pp. 109–169. Springer, New York (2011)
3. Mommers, L.: Ontologies in the legal domain. In: Poli, R., Seibt, J. (eds.) Theory and Applications of Ontology: Philosophical Perspectives, pp. 265–276. Springer, Dordrecht (2010)
4. Engers, T., Boer, A., Breuker, J., Valente, A., Winkels, R.: Ontologies in the legal domain. In: Chen, H., Brandt, L., Gregg, V., Traunmüller, R., Dawes, S., Hovy, E., Macintosh, A., Larson, C. (eds.) Digital Government, pp. 233–261. Springer, New York (2008)

---

[1] http://www.wcoomd.org

5. Melz, E., Valente, A.: Modeling the tax code. In: Meersman, R., Tari, Z., Corsaro, A. (eds.) OTM-WS 2004. LNCS, vol. 3292, pp. 652–661. Springer, Heidelberg (2004)
6. Buranarach, M., Thein, Y.M., Supnithi, T.: A community-driven approach to development of an ontology-based application management framework. In: Takeda, H., Qu, Y., Mizoguchi, R., Kitamura, Y. (eds.) JIST 2012. LNCS, vol. 7774, pp. 306–312. Springer, Heidelberg (2013)
7. Apache Jena - Reasoners and rule engines Jena inference support. http://jena.apache.org/documentation/inference
8. Bizer, C.: D2R MAP - a database to RDF mapping language. In: Proceedings of the 12th International World Wide Web Conference (WWW 2003) (2003)

Earth Observation Data Interoperability Arrangement with Vocabulary Registry

Masahiko Nagai[1(✉)], Ashik Rajbhandari[1], Masafumi Ono[2], and Ryosuke Shibaski[2]

[1] Asian Institute of Technology,
km 42, Paholyothin Highway, P.O. Box 4, Klong Luang,
Pathumthani 12120, Thailand
nagaim@ait.ac.th
[2] University of Tokyo, Cw-503, IIS, 4-6-1, Komaba,
Meguro-ku, Tokyo 153-8505, Japan

Abstract. Standardization organizations are working for syntactic and schematic level of interoperability. At the same time, semantic interoperability should be considered as heterogeneous conditions and also very diversified with a large-volume data. The vocabulary registry has been developed and ontological information such as technical vocabularies for earth observation has been collected for data interoperability arrangement. This is a very challenging method for earth observation data interoperability because collaboration or cooperation with scientists of different disciplines is essential for common understanding. SKOS-editor is developed to register and update technical vocabularies as a part of the vocabulary registry, which promises to be a useful tool for users to handle SKOS format. In order to invite contributions from the user community, it is necessary to provide sophisticated and easy-to-use tools. Registered vocabularies supply the reference information required for earth observation data retrieval. We proposed data/metadata search with ontology such as technical vocabularies and visualization of relations among dataset to very large scale and various earth observation data.

Keywords: Ontology · Data interoperability · SKOS · Earth observation data

1 Introduction

Utilization of earth observation data is lying on trans-disciplinary fields, such as hydrology, geology, geography, agriculture, biology, disaster, remote sensing, GIS, and so on. It is essential to cross these trans-disciplinary fields for effective use of earth observation data and to measure the global environmental problems, such as climate change, global worming, various disasters, and so on. One of the key issues is data interoperability arrangement under the trans-disciplinary conditions. There are two aspects of the data interoperability: syntactic interoperability and semantic interoperability. Improvement of both aspects of interoperability is needed for integrated use of heterogeneous data. To improve the syntax interoperability, many efforts have already been made such as standardization of data formats and development of

A. Kawtrakul et al. (Eds.): ISIP 2013, CCIS 421, pp. 128–136, 2014.
DOI: 10.1007/978-3-319-08732-0_10, © Springer International Publishing Switzerland 2014

XML-based data encoding rules, for example, ISO (International Organization for Standardization) standard and OGC (Open Geospatial Consortium) standard. De facto standards are also recognized as well. On the other hand, improvement of semantic interoperability requires common understanding among different ontologies, terminologies, taxonomies, including definitions and associations of various concepts/terms, name spaces, classification schemes and so on, which is collectively called an "ontology". The word "ontology" was originally used in philosophy, to refer to the branch of metaphysics that deals with the nature of being. Currently, in context of knowledge sharing, the term means a specification of a conceptualization [1]. In recent years, several institutions have initiated efforts to propose a standard ontology and/or terminology/taxonomy related with Earth Observation. SWEET (Semantic Web for Environment and Technology) by NASA (National Aeronautics and Space Administration) is one such ontology [2]. FAO (Food and Agriculture Organization of the United Nations) is making similar kinds of efforts based on AGROVOC, that is s a multilingual, structured and controlled vocabulary designed to cover the terminology of all subject fields in agriculture, forestry, fisheries, food and related domains [3]. Many other ontologies and terminologies/taxonomies are expected to be proposed by other expert/professional communities and institutions. For data interoperability, ontological information including technical vocabularies, terminology, taxonomy, glossary, etc., should be collected, managed, referred and compared; for example, data dictionaries, classification schemata, terminologies, thesauruses, and their relations are handled. Common understanding of heterogeneous semantic information is used for data sharing and data services such as supporting data retrieval, metadata design, information mining, and so on.

In this study, the vocabulary registry has been developed by using a Semantic MediaWiki, which helps to gather ontological information and associations for data interoperability among diversified and distributed data sources in the field of earth observation. Generally, ontology is applied to a strict and well-defined purpose, classes and instances such as task ontology [4], but in this study, the scope of ontologies is not restricted and comprises any reference information based on technical vocabularies of various domains. Registered vocabularies can be converted to RDF or SKOS format to share with various user communities. SKOS editor is also developed to modify ontological information. A technical vocabulary is extremely an essential lexicon for the knowledge seekers that helps them to understand the facts giving clear picture about the ambiguous terminologies. Any vocabulary is effective only when they provide substantial benefits to its users as accepted by everyone for its useful purposes. The vocabulary registry creates a "knowledge writing tool" for experts, by extracting semantic relations from authoritative documents using natural language processing techniques, such as morphological analysis and semantic analysis for earth observation data interoperability of DIAS (Data Integration and Analysis System).

DIAS is a Japanese national key project having missions to archive such earth environmental data and then to analyse global phenomenon through combining and processing these data such as observation data, numerical model outputs, and socio-economic data provided from the fields of climate, water cycle, ecosystem, ocean, biodiversity and agriculture. The aim of DIAS is to share earth observation data and knowledge among different disciplines. Currently, many researchers in the science and engineering fields are participating in DIAS. DIAS is one of GEOSS (Global Earth Observation System of Systems) activities in Japan.

2 Vocabulary Registry

In order to collect vocabulary, a registration system is developed based on Semantic MediaWiki. Semantic MediaWiki is a feature-rich wiki implementation. Semantic MediaWiki handles hyperlinks and has simple text syntax for creating new pages and cross-links between terms [5]. Entry words, definitions, sources, and authors are handled as nodes with tags, and relations to other terms are handled as links. Those terms are surrounded by other relational vocabularies. Here, each ontologies or vocabularies are managed by separate Wikis.

2.1 Vocabulary Registration

At first, vocabularies are added to Semantic MediaWiki by the developed tool automatically converting form text, spreadsheet, RDF, and OWL to XML and importing to Wiki. Sometimes, vocabularies are manually registered from books and Web pages. These existing dictionaries or glossaries are already considered as ontological information. Table 1 shows vocabulary sources from existing glossaries which is used for this study. OCR (Optical character reader) is sometimes used to digitize the legacy sources. Secondly, symbols and abbreviations, such as related words and synonyms are extracted from the dictionary and converted from semantic structure to syntactic structure by natural language processing. Finally, imported ontological information is modified by authorized users with editing function of the Wiki as shown in Fig. 1.

Table 1. Vocabulary sources from existing glossaries

No.	Name	Language	Data format
1	WMO glossary	English	Web pages
2	CEOS Missions, Instruments and Measurements(MIM) Database	English	MS Excel
3	CEOS System Engineering Office(SEO)	English	MS Excel
4	GEMET	English	RDF
5	INSPIRE Feature Concept Dictionary	English	Web pages
6	SWEET	English	OWL
7	CUASHSI	English	OWL
8	CF Standard Names	English	Web pages
9	GCMD	English	Web pages
10	Eurovoc Theasaurus	English	Web pages
11	International Glossary of Hydrology/UNESCO	English	Web pages
12	Marine Metadata Interoperability	English	Web pages

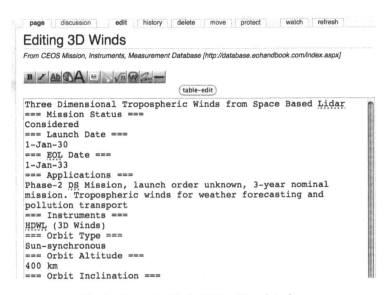

Fig. 1. Semantic Media Wiki editing interface

In Semantic MediaWiki, a visual depiction of content is expressed by tags. It is not easy to add or select appropriate relations by tags without knowledge of computer science and miss spelling, so in this study, we developed a table like editor as a wiki plug-in. The table editor links to editing page of the Wiki by pop-up window and suggest appropriate tags to control community authoring. The table editor is implemented by dhtmlGrid standard. XML is prepared for Web server. Figure 2 shows Semantic MediaWiki table editor, by which the user can browse and edit explanations

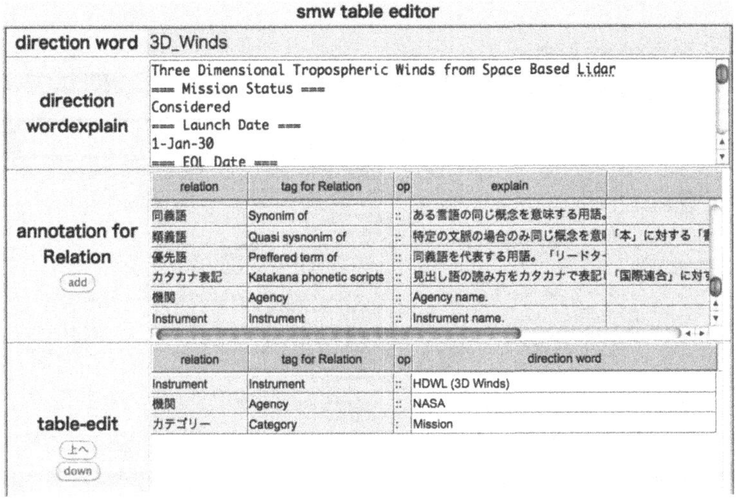

Fig. 2. Semantic MediaWiki table editor

of a term without ambiguity of tags. Semantic Media Wiki displays not only defini-tions, but also relations of terms among multiple Wikis. The table editor is applied in order to modify relations of terms by using a table without tags.

2.2 Vocabulary Retrieval

Registered vocabularies that are stored in each Semantic MediaWiki are retrieved all together by the reverse dictionary. The reverse dictionary describes a concept of a term from definitions and associations of terms. The reverse dictionary is developed based on GETA (Generic Engine for Transposable Association), which was developed by the National Institute of Informatics, Japan [6]. It comprises tools for manipulating large-dimensional sparse matrices for text retrieval through more than one Wiki in all together. GETA is an engine for the calculation of associations such as similarity measurement of multiple Wikis. In order to create matrices to find similarity, mor-phological analysis is conducted for word segmentation and listing of ignored words for calculation of associations. For example, the query is "earth environment obser-vation by satellite or air-craft". The result is "remote sensing". The reverse dictionary relates data by calculation of similarity by using a definition. The user without basic knowledge can discover the specific technical vocabularies that are linked to earth observation data. The reverse dictionary can be directly used to realize associative searching systems, which accept a group of texts as queries, and return highly related texts in the relevance order.

2.3 Graphical Representation

In order to compare associations among the different keywords from various existing glossaries, graph representation as shown in Fig. 3 is useful to understand their relations visually. The result of vocabulary retrieval is represented visually. Also,

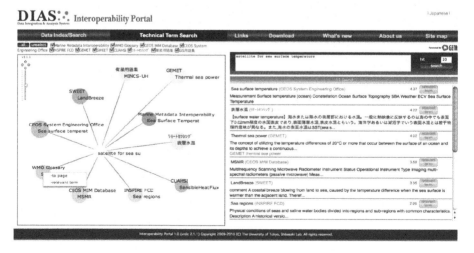

Fig. 3. Graph representation for reverse dictionary with Wiki

broader, narrower or related concept are visually represented. The graph representation is developed by KeyGraph that is open source of Java library. XML data that is constructed in the Wiki is visualized with the result of information retrieval by the reverse dictionary. All the related terms from various vocabularies are represented at once. Graph representation proves a clear association between the two vocabularies. Then, those associations are treated as newly-created ontological information, and is added through the Semantic MediaWiki. The ontological information can grow autonomously by adding relations, becoming more and more useful.

3   SKOS Editor

There is a great need of such vocabulary registry that maintains the quality of semantic interoperability at high level implementing various appropriate methods, tools and open standards. SKOS is applicable for indexing and retrieval of vocabularies [7]. Therefore, web-based SKOS editor is developed using the open source SKOS API provided by SourceForge, as shown in Fig. 4.

The controlled vocabulary generated by the SKOS editor is fully compatible with the W3C's semantic web standards (SKOS). It comes with several basic essential features in order to satisfy with the SKOS model such as inclusion of the basic structure and content of concept schemes such as thesauri, classification schemes, subject heading lists, taxonomies, folksonomies, and other similar types of controlled vocabulary (W3C SKOS primer). After a successful login authentication, the users can play around with the concepts and their inter-relational hierarchy. The users can define any broader, narrower or related concept with its appropriate literals, axioms or definitions easily; and update, edit or delete them as per their requirement at the same time. In this way, the SKOS editor can therefore be very useful in bringing the common understanding of various knowledge seekers together into common ground, which helps to validate and upgrade the vocabulary in collaborative approach.

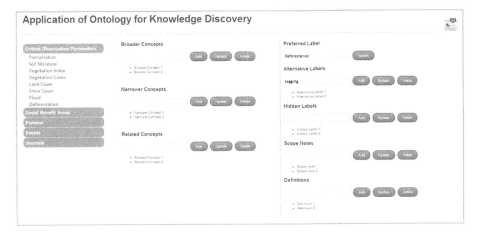

Fig. 4. SKOS editor web-based interface

4 Implementation of Vocabulary Registry

DIAS is tackling a large increase in volume of the earth observation data. DIAS has been developing a core system for data integration and analysis that includes the supporting functions of life cycle data management, data search, information exploration, scientific analysis, and partial data downloading. DIAS is also tackling a large increase in diversity of the earth observation data. For improving data interoperability, DIAS is developing a system for identifying the relationship between data by using ontology on technical terms and ideas, and geography. DIAS also is acquiring database information from various sources by developing a cross-sectoral search engine. Interoperability portal for DIAS has been developed. This portal provides metadata search with various vocabularies. It shows visualization of relation s among dataset to very large scale and various earth observation data registered in the DIAS core system.

Earth observation data has spatial and temporal attributes such as the geographic coverage and the time stamp of data creation with scientific keywords. The metadata standard is published by the geographic information technical committee (TC211) in ISO 19115 and 19139 series. Accordingly, DIAS metadata is developed based on ISO/TC211 metadata standards. From the viewpoint of data users, metadata is useful not only for data retrieval and analysis but also for interoperability and information sharing among experts. In DIAS, document centric metadata registration tool has been developed for reducing time for creating metadata. Since various kinds of datasets stored in DIAS increase, it is necessary to support searching datasets based on keywords, spatial conditions, and temporal conditions with created metadata. This vocabulary registry is utilized for keywords control of DIAS metadata. It means that

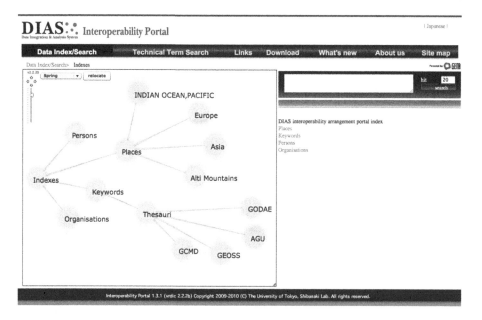

Fig. 5. Index of data search with ontology

associations of data can be shown as associations of keywords. Datasets are classified into some categories based on such criteria as GCMD Science Keywords or GEOSS social benefit areas [8].

Registered metadata and scientific keyword vocabularies are managed in the DIAS interoperability portal. Figure 5 shows the index of data retrieval approach. Dataset is accessed from four categories, persons, places, keywords, and organization as well. Persons are the responsible person name for dataset. Places are the location of dataset such as country and city name. Organization is the information of data provider. Keywords are the related metadata that are controlled by vocabulary registry. The DIAS interoperability portal helps keyword retrieval to specify from broader term to narrower term. The result shows not only related dataset but also related researchers name, organization, and available location of dataset.

5   Conclusions

According to the improvement of observation technologies and earth science studies, a large amount and various kinds of earth observation data including remote sensing data, in situ data, GIS data and model simulation data are globally being produced by many experts and researchers. At the same time, many kinds of ontology, glossaries, thesauruses, and gazetteers are being used in various fields. The vocabulary registry needs to be developed as a showcase and as a basis for the comparative analysis for better semantic interoperability among diversified earth observation data. The vocabulary registry is carrying out a component of DIAS interoperability infrastructure through the keyword list of DIAS metadata.

We have developed the vocabulary registry and collected the authoritative vocabularies, glossaries, dictionaries, terminologies and ontologies about the earth observation domain and also developed the multi-referential reverse dictionary including them. Ontological information, such as technical vocabulary is extremely an essential lexicon for the knowledge seekers that helps them to understand the facts giving clear picture about the ambiguous terminologies. Registered vocabularies can be converted to RDF or SKOS format to share with various user communities. SKOS editor has been developed to modify ontological information. The reverse dictionary supports getting unknown meanings from our own vocabularies as well as being linked various earth observation dataset. We have closely worked with user community of DIAS and often update vocabularies and metadata by the request of users. Our proposed approach is beneficial for earth observation data interoperability management with vocabularies.

References

1. Smith, B.: Preprint version of chapter, Ontology. In: Floridi, L. (ed.) Blackwell Guide to the Philosophy of Computing and Information. Blackwell, Oxford (2003)
2. Roskin, R., Pan, M.: Knowledge representation in the semantic web for Earth and environmental terminology (SWEET). Comput. Geosci. 31(9), 1119–1125 (2005)

3. Sini, M., Luser, B., Salokhe, G., Keizer, J., Katz, S.: The AGROVOC concept server: rationale, goals and usage. Libr. Rev. **57**(3), 200–212 (2007)
4. Kitamura, Y., Kashiwase, M., Fuse, M., Mizoguchi, R.: Deployment of an ontological framework of functional design knowledge. Adv. Eng. Inform. **18**(2), 115–129 (2004)
5. Herzig, D.M., Ell, B.: Semantic MediaWiki in operation: experiences with building a semantic portal. In: Patel-Schneider, P.F., Pan, Y., Hitzler, P., Mika, P., Zhang, L., Pan, J.Z., Horrocks, I., Glimm, B. (eds.) ISWC 2010, Part II. LNCS, vol. 6497, pp. 114–128. Springer, Heidelberg (2010)
6. Takano, A., Niwa, Y., Nishioka, S., Iwayama, M., Hisamitsu, T., Imaichi, O., Sakurai, H.: Information access based on associative calculation. In: Jeffery, K., Hlaváč, V., Wiedermann, J. (eds.) SOFSEM 2000. LNCS, vol. 1963, pp. 187–201. Springer, Heidelberg (2000)
7. van Assem, M., Malaisé, V., Miles, A., Schreiber, G.: A method to convert thesauri to SKOS. In: Sure, Y., Domingue, J. (eds.) ESWC 2006. LNCS, vol. 4011, pp. 95–109. Springer, Heidelberg (2006)
8. Greene, S., Tanin, E., Plaisant, C., Shneiderman, B., Olsen, L., Major, G., Johns, S.: The end of zero-hit queries: query previews for NASA's global change master directory. Int. J. Digit. Libr. **2**(2–3), 79–90 (1999)

Author Index